TEXAS
ADOPTION
ACTIVIST

EDNA GLADNEY

TEXAS ADOPTION ACTIVIST

EDNA GLADNEY

A LIFE & LEGACY OF *Love*

SHERRIE S. McLEROY

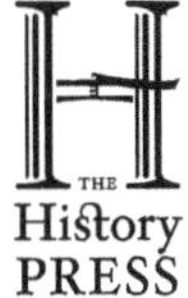

Published by The History Press
Charleston, SC 29403
www.historypress.net

First published 2014

Manufactured in the United States

ISBN 978.1.62619.351.2

Library of Congress CIP data applied for.

Notice: The information in this book is true and complete to the best of our knowledge. It is offered without guarantee on the part of the author or The History Press. The author and The History Press disclaim all liability in connection with the use of this book.

This book is gratefully dedicated to Jane Dumas Chester (1926–2006), Deb Chester Maclin, Mary Owen Routh and Kathy Steel Ferber, who so generously shared their Aunt Edna with me; to my mother, Shirley Penny Snead (1933–2011); and to my own "Gladney baby," Ann Elizabeth McLeRoy.

CONTENTS

Acknowledgements

Finding Edna Gladney's true story has consumed years of my life and a lot of space in my office. And there are parts of it I am still trying to document. The length of this book required condensing or even leaving out many people and events that I hope to cover in future volumes.

One note about my descriptions of Edna's legislative campaigns: Texas adoption laws are very complex and have been revised many times—only to be expected, I suppose, since it was one of the first three states to even pass such laws (1856). I don't pretend to be anywhere near an expert on the subject, so I have simplified them considerably and tried to show them from Edna's viewpoint. She left some very candid notes and letters about her impatience with the entire process and with legislators who just didn't get the point.

A history as complex as Edna's isn't written in a vacuum, and there are many people I'd like to thank. First and foremost is her family in Fort Worth: Deb Chester Maclin, her daughter Misty Gober and Deb's mother, the late Jane Dumas Chester, all of whom opened their hearts and shared Edna with me. Deb even lets me borrow one of her aunt's hats and a purse still stained inside with her signature purple ink when I give talks about the Aunt Edna she had the good fortune to know as a child. I was also lucky enough to track down several of Edna's Milwaukee cousins: the marvelous Mary Owen Routh, her sister Virginia Loock and their niece Kathy Steel Ferber. Mary was delegated by the family to tell me the true story of Edna's birth, which almost literally knocked me out of my chair and then made so much sense. Knowing that one truth makes so many of Edna's actions perfectly understandable.

A big thank you to the Cuchara Association of Lady Writers—you know who you are—who helped me get Edna back on track more than once. And special blessings to my friend and colleague Ruth Karbach, who got as much of a charge out of finding stuff on Edna as I did.

Many thanks to the staff of the Gladney Center for Adoption, past and present, who supported this project: Ginna Baker, Pattye Hicks, Nonya Jordan, Jennifer Lanter, Wendy Lee, Mike McMahon, Nancy Robbins and Ellen Wilson. Thank you all for your trust.

Thank you to the professionals, archives and libraries where I have done research: Milwaukee County Historical Society; Milwaukee Public Library; Brenda McClurkin and Cathy Spitzenberger in Special Collections at the University of Texas at Arlington; Betty Shankle, Donna Cruse and Kathryn Cain in the Genealogy and Local History section of the Fort Worth Public Library; Susan Pritchett and Dr. Dawn Youngblood at Tarrant County Archives; Jackie Banfield at Sherman Public Library; Marcia Rolbiecki at Red River Historical Museum; Shonkista Stephens with the City of Sherman; Texas Collection at Baylor University; Calvin Scott, Central Texas Conference of United Methodist Church Archives; Nancy Sparrow, Alexander Architectural Archives, University of Texas Libraries; Ned Comstock at the University of Southern California's Cinematic Arts Library; Bruce Pfeiffer, Frank Lloyd Wright Foundation; La Grange (Illinois) Historical Society; Vicki Hansen, National Association of Social Workers/Texas; Aryn Glazier and Margaret Schlankey, Dolph Briscoe Center for American History, University of Texas; Matt Dewaelsche, San Antonio Public Library/Archives; and Nicci Hester, Southwest Collection, Texas Tech University.

Thanks also to Shannon Fifer, of Warner Brothers Motion Picture Rights Intellectual Property, who generously gave me permission to use stills from *Blossoms in the Dust*; Pat Sinker, who provided material on the Women's Service League; William Penn for information on his mother, Addilee Abell; and Fort Worth Camera Shop.

If I forgot to list you, please forgive me—it's hard to remember everyone you've communicated with over ten years.

And as always, my love and thanks to Bill and Ann, who live with an author without killing her. Bill is my historical fact checker and my first editor—and we're still married. Love to you both.

And thank you, Edna Gladney, for making our lives—and those of so many other people—happy.

Introduction

In early April 1940, Edna Browning Kahly Gladney of Fort Worth, Texas, received a letter that would change not only her life but also those of thousands of unborn children.

Hollywood's Metro-Goldwyn-Mayer Studios wanted to make a movie about her.

"What on earth could anybody write about me?" she asked. Quite a bit, as it turned out, and her larger-than-life story helped move adoption from the secrecy that had shrouded it into the light of public acceptance.

Edna's "reel" story began some months earlier when MGM screenwriter and publicist Ralph Wheelwright and his wife, Phinie Louise, decided to adopt a child. They began their search at the Cradle in Evanston, Illinois, but didn't find a child who touched their hearts. So they traveled to Fort Worth, where the Texas Children's Home and Aid Society (TCHAS) had been securing homes and "bright futures" for orphaned, dependent and neglected children for fifty years.

There they met Edna Gladney, the organization's short, plump, vivacious and fashionable superintendent. She fit no one's image of a plain, soberly dressed, grim maternity/adoption home matron, nor was her facility a white and sterile institution. To the contrary, Edna declared, "if any place on earth should be light [and] gay...surely a children's home should." And the same, in her opinion, applied to its administrator.

The TCHAS facility at 1315 West El Paso Street, in a quiet and tree-shaded neighborhood of older residences near downtown Fort Worth, was literally a home—a turn-of-the-twentieth-century house filled with Edna's own furniture and belongings. Bright chintz and lace curtains, comfortable mahogany chairs and sofas, family photos and flowers filled the rooms. Even the nursery ceiling was papered with blue morning glories so the babies would have something to look at as they lay in their cribs. Every room had rocking chairs, as Edna believed that "it takes a lot of rocking to make up for not having a mother."

Like so many before them, the Wheelwrights had not only "come home" but found their new daughter, too, a toddler they also named Phinie Louise.

Intrigued by Edna, Ralph, a former newspaperman, delved into her history and that of the Home, discovering that the widowed Edna was childless herself. Though lively and friendly, she had the heart of a crusader who had spent years campaigning to eliminate the cruel designation of "illegitimate" on Texas birth certificates. Why? Because Edna Gladney was illegitimate, too, a then shameful secret that she shared with few.

And by the time she met Ralph, Edna had embarked on another mission: transforming the TCHAS from a Victorian institution that only placed children in homes to a modern adoption agency that also operated a maternity home for unwed mothers—a daring plan that led many to brand her as encouraging immorality.

Ralph realized he had found a story worthy of a movie.

He returned to Los Angeles and pitched his idea to studio head Louis B. Mayer as *the* movie to follow in the footsteps of MGM's successful *Boys Town*. Mayer agreed and saw Edna's story of personal tragedy and triumph as the kind of nostalgia that movie audiences wanted to escape the tensions of the European war and its looming impact on the United States.

But Edna was interested because the movie would give her a platform to talk about several important children's issues, both in this country and abroad.

So, with the understanding that Ralph would hide her illicit origin, she said "yes" to MGM, and *Blossoms in the Dust* went into production.

Chapter 1

FINDING THE STORY

Though the film follows the chronology of the Texas Children's Home and Aid Society only in connection with Edna's life, its actual history began long before she was involved.

The Home's origins dated to 1887, when a loose confederation of Fort Worth women's groups became interested in helping homeless and dependent children. Because the city was an important railroad hub, many babies were abandoned on trains or in depots. Hundreds more over the years were left in deserted lots, on empty streets and in boardinghouses or were rescued from "baby farms," much like today's puppy mills. To salvage more, the Woman's Christian Temperance Union (WCTU) even invaded "Hell's Half Acre," the city's notorious saloon and red-light district, where children lived with their mothers or scratched out a living on the streets. By 1891, the women had established the Fort Worth Benevolent Home, an orphanage appropriately housed in a former brothel.

THE MAN WITH THE BASKET

That was also the year that the Reverend Isaac Zachary Taylor Morris, a Methodist minister, was transferred to Fort Worth's City Mission. As part of his church work, he, too, looked out for needy children in the poor, squalid sections and worked with the temperance ladies in the "Acre."

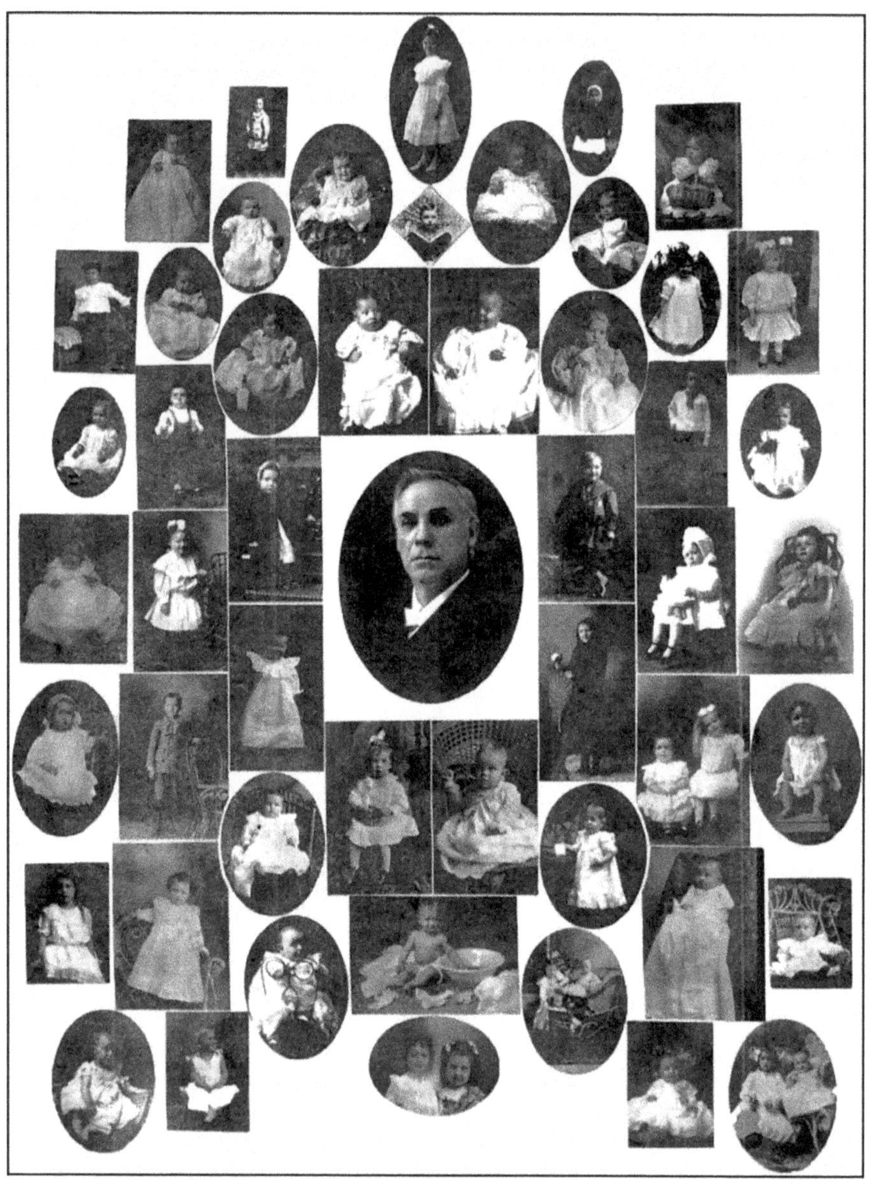

Reverend I.Z.T. Morris and some of the "waifs" for whom he found homes and brighter futures. *Central Texas Conference of United Methodist Church Archives.*

In 1896, the Chicago-based National Children's Home Society opened a Texas branch with headquarters in Fort Worth and named WCTU member and Fort Worth Benevolent Home director Belle Burchill as superintendent.

Unlike the traditional orphanage, the TCHAS did not "warehouse" children until they reached adulthood but placed them as quickly as possible with a new family and home. If the child was formally adopted, so much the better; but most of them were not full orphans, making a legal solution difficult. The main goal was to provide carefully selected homes, a good education and a decent, preferably Christian, upbringing.

Several months later, Burchill returned to her position with the Fort Worth Benevolent Home, and Reverend Morris was asked by the national society to head the fledgling TCHAS. He accepted, even though the work would be in addition to his ministerial position and meant raising funds for the organization as well as conducting its rescue work.

Thanks to free passes often given to charities by railroad companies, Morris traveled throughout Texas and the Southwest locating children in need, taking others to new homes and checking on previous placements. Because he usually transported infants in baskets, he became known as "the man with the basket," who frequently broke into spirited hymns on the long rail journeys.

He and his wife, Belle, bought a large two-story house in 1902 in the Polytechnic College section of Fort Worth for their own seven children, plus varying numbers of TCHAS babies and children who stayed there while awaiting placement. Much of that work fell to Belle and her daughters, who

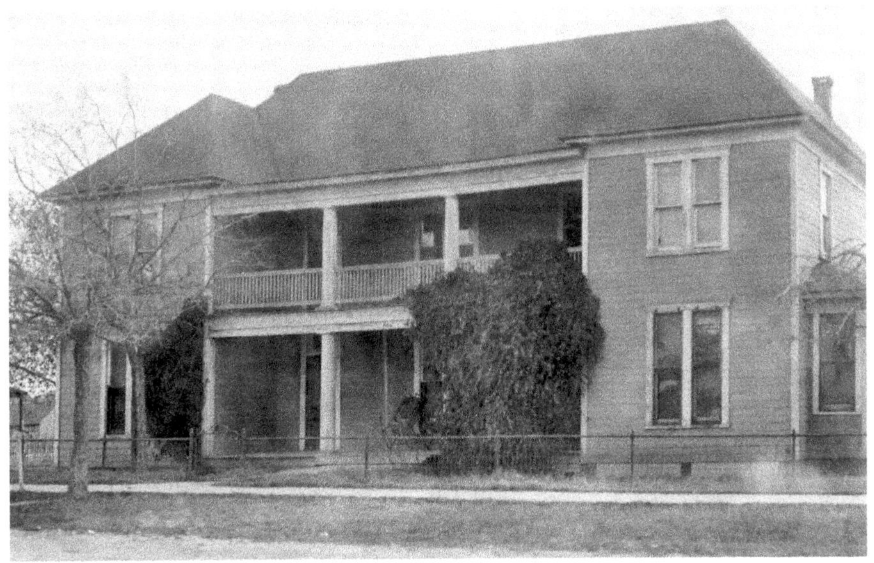

The Morris residence also housed children waiting to be placed in new homes. Fort Worth Star-Telegram *Collection, Special Collections, University of Texas–Arlington.*

never knew if they would be caring for a few or several dozen babies and youngsters.

Morris used city newspapers throughout Texas to spread the word about available children whom he was ready to place as *family* members, "not as servants, nor as boarders." He often adjured readers to "create bright futures" for these "street waifs" by opening their homes and hearts to them.

His efforts were colorblind despite the prevalent racism and bigotry of the day. He took in and placed Hispanic and African American children, ever vigilant that they not be used as servants. As more Central and Eastern European immigrant workers came to the booming Fort Worth stockyards area, Morris maintained a watch over their children, too, as many of those families lived in abject poverty.

He found that the most difficult child to place was the nursing infant; most applications were for children at least two years old. No one, including orphanages, wanted the babies. "Well, I know they seem to be less trouble at that [older] age," Morris grumbled, "but the poor little orphan baby needs a home as bad as the boy 6 years old."[1] This problem would not be solved until infant formula was developed in the 1920s.

MESSAGES OF PAIN AND LOVE

The Gladney Center for Adoption archives hold several dozen surviving letters to Morris and his wife from adoptees, birth mothers and adoptive parents such as this couple, rejoicing in their new family: "She is the sweetest baby you ever put your hands upon. If you had traveled as far as man could go, I feel in my heart that you could not have found a baby to fill our hearts with love for it like this one."

Children placed by the Morrises wrote "to let you know how I am getting along…Mother [Belle Morris] I love yall yet…I'll never forget your kindness. Mother I am glad to tell you I am well pleased with my home."

Several letters bore painful news, reflecting the high infant mortality rates of the time. "The baby is now as fat as she can be, in fine health…words cannot express our love for it." Less than four months later, "I am very sorry to tell you that our baby is dead…we done everything in our power for we loved her…it seems like she just crept into our hearts before we knew it."

Equally heart-wrenching were letters from birth mothers, usually young, single and condemned to ostracism and the lowest rungs of society if word of their shame leaked out. "I arrived at home [from Fort Worth]...and Oh! You don't know how I miss my dear little babe. I want to hear [about] her so bad...Write and tell me about my Darling babe, for my god I don't see how I can bear it." Another "lonely Broken hearted mother" wanted to know if her daughter was dead or alive and what had become of her.

Building an Institution

Reverend Morris waged a constant battle for enough money to operate and enough room to house the children. To augment funds, he placed "glass banks"—glass jars—in businesses and railroad ticket offices around Fort Worth and wrote endless letters to supporters.

By 1904, however, he was so strapped for money and assistance that he agreed to charter the Texas Children's Home and Aid Society with the state, hoping that a larger and more formal organization would succeed. Alone, Morris had placed more than six hundred children, four hundred of them in Texas. Despite the cost, he had gone wherever he was called, including to sites of natural disasters that left behind many orphans. The Great Galveston (Texas) Storm of 1900, still America's single greatest loss of life outside of war, posed one of his biggest challenges: more than six thousand people had died.

Morris also pushed for legislative reforms, and among his causes was punishment of parents who deserted their children. He noted that, of the six hundred children he'd placed, only fifty or so were true orphans; the rest had been abandoned. Morris advocated as well for establishment of juvenile courts and a statewide rescue facility for women in need. He was impatient with the rigid hierarchies with which he often had to deal, believing that too many institutions had been ruined by being "organized to death."

Reverend Morris dedicated his life to lost children, working until only days before his death in December 1914.

A New Era

Belle Morris followed her husband as superintendent of TCHAS. Fifty-seven years old and worn from working by her husband's side for decades, Belle struggled on into her mid-sixties before agreeing to semi-retire. World

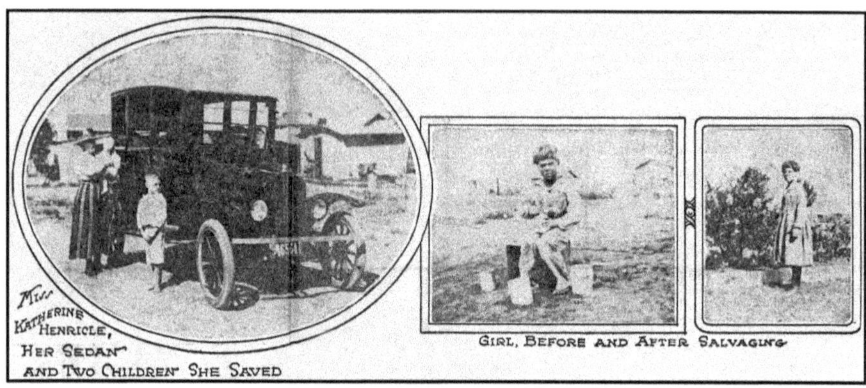

In the booming Texas oil fields, many children lived in poverty and filth, as seen in this photo titled "Salvaging the Oil Field Waifs" in the *Fort Worth Star-Telegram* of August 21, 1921.

War I had been a boon to Fort Worth, attracting railroad, meatpacking, oil field and construction workers by the thousands from across the country. But for the Texas Children's Home, that growth also meant more children in need, especially in its Wichita Falls branch office with its nearby oil fields.

Worse, donations had flattened after Reverend Morris's death. Now in severe financial distress, the Home resorted to low-yielding special events, hired "aviators" to fly over Fort Worth's business district and drop flyers about the need for funds and displayed available babies in the window of Pemberton Furniture Store.

Social work was a new profession in 1921, and the old Victorian institutions that had pioneered charitable work in the United States were either adopting modern ideas and organization or fading quietly out of existence. Belle Morris and the board of directors realized it was time for them to also change: professionally trained staff members were the first step.

Roy Stockwell was a college graduate who had studied philanthropy and social work. After serving in World War I and being gassed at Verdun, he returned to his chosen work and was with the Houston Anti-Tuberculosis League when the Texas Children's Home hired him, first as a field agent and then as superintendent. Stockwell promptly hired a colleague, H. Wirt Steele, to become its financial and publicity manager.

They faced monumental problems in the fifteen districts and offices around the state, especially in Fort Worth, which was now glutted with thousands of idle workers, many of them from Mexico. The plight of those children touched many hearts, and when Mrs. Baird's Bakery produced a "monster" cake weighing one thousand pounds, a number of civic clubs, working through TCHAS, purchased it for the children of the Valley View neighborhood on the Trinity River. "The huge cake was decorated with small pink sugar rosebuds," reported the *Fort Worth Star-Telegram*. "When these were broken [off] and given to the little Mexican girls, their eyes brightened and they smiled in wonder and admiration. Holding the rosebuds carefully, they looked at them long and not one of them ate her rosebud."[2]

But most of the Home's problems were not so sweetly solved. Stockwell and Steel canvassed the state in search of funds and placed ads in newspapers: "Prosperity is beginning again in Texas—but that does not mean the needs of the poor have all been met, or [that] the opportunity for charitable giving has disappeared."[3] Their workload, said Stockwell, had increased 200 percent because of new social welfare regulations to keep children with their birth families if at all possible. The organization desperately needed a new receiving facility, where children could be kept until placed with new families or returned to their own. But to build it and carry on operations would cost nearly $50,000, the equivalent today of well over half a million dollars. Where was the money to come from?

Roy Stockwell and the TCHAS didn't know it, but help—in a very unlikely form—was on the way.

Chapter 2

A Whirlwind from Milwaukee

Edna Browning Jones was born in Milwaukee, Wisconsin, on January 22, 1886, the daughter of Minnie Nell Jones, an unwed mother barely seventeen years old. And Edna's father? Probably a British sailor, but no one knows for certain. In the twenty-first century, "illegitimacy" no longer carries the scandal and stigma that it did in 1886—in part, ironically, because of Edna's work. But children born like her, out of wedlock, had long been branded as inferior both in society and on official documents. As late as the mid-twentieth century, some states' birth certificates still bluntly proclaimed them as illegitimate, a brand that could never be erased and followed them all their lives.

Seven years after Edna's birth, Minnie married Maurice Kahly, a sales clerk nine years her senior who gave Edna his name and soon also gave her a half-sister, Dorothy.

Their life in Milwaukee was not the privileged one depicted in *Blossoms in the Dust*, but it was comfortable and middle-class. By the time her sister was born, Edna was already well-established on her charitable course. "How did this come about?" the *Woman's Home Companion* asked Dorothy Kahly Dumas in a 1954 article. "As naturally as sunshine," Dumas replied. "It was Edna's nature to worry about other people—particularly about other people's children—even when she was a child herself. From the time she was a five-year-old she brought ragamuffins in off the streets to bathe and dress them."[4]

At school, the striking blue-eyed brunette with alabaster skin and an infectious smile was known for her elegant penmanship and collection

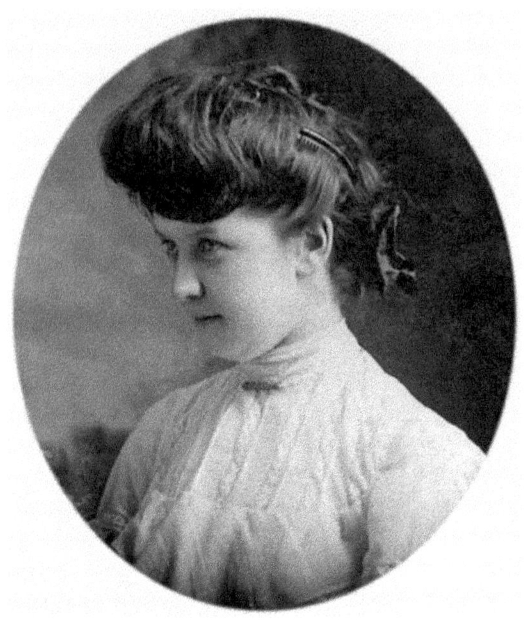

of friendship lockets. A classmate told television's *This Is Your Life* host Ralph Edwards in 1953 that Edna's hobby was making friends. Her school's location near the Milwaukee Infants' Home also helped reinforce her budding career of benevolence. "I love…the little foundling home," she told the *Milwaukee Journal* in 1941. "I really learned much about the care of children from the loving attention the babies receive there. In fact, my inspiration and love for children was born there."

Sometime around 1900, Edna's life began to change. She suffered a serious illness, never specified by her but probably respiratory. After three years of high school, she went to work as a clerk for the Mutual Life Insurance Company to help support her sister and mother, who periodically

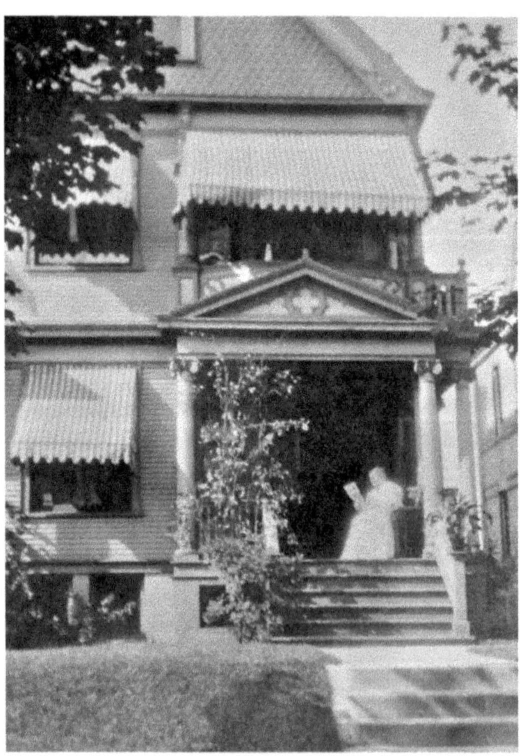

Top: Edna as a young schoolgirl in Milwaukee. *Deb Chester Maclin.*

Left: Edna's grandmother Rachel Jones on the porch of her Milwaukee home. *Deb Chester Maclin.*

separated from her husband, Maurice Kahly. And even when Minnie was living with him, Edna usually resided with her Grandmother Jones. Her relationship with Kahly was sporadic after that. She rarely spoke of him in later years other than to make his career seem more important than it was. And as soon as she married in 1906, she ceased using his name, signing herself for the rest of her life as Edna B. (Browning) Gladney.

Gone to Texas

In the fall of 1904, Minnie sent Edna to Fort Worth, Texas, to stay with Minnie's sister Flora Jones Goetz, brother-in-law Arthur Goetz and niece Florence. Ostensibly, it was her hope that a drier and less polluted climate would help Edna's health problems, but Minnie may have also wanted to give Edna a "leg up" in society that she wouldn't have in Milwaukee. Arthur Goetz was an executive with industrialist Edgar Marston's New York–based Texas & Pacific Coal Company and was prominent in Fort Worth's business and civic circles. T&P's Thurber Brick Company, which Goetz headed, had helped erect the meatpacking plants of Swift

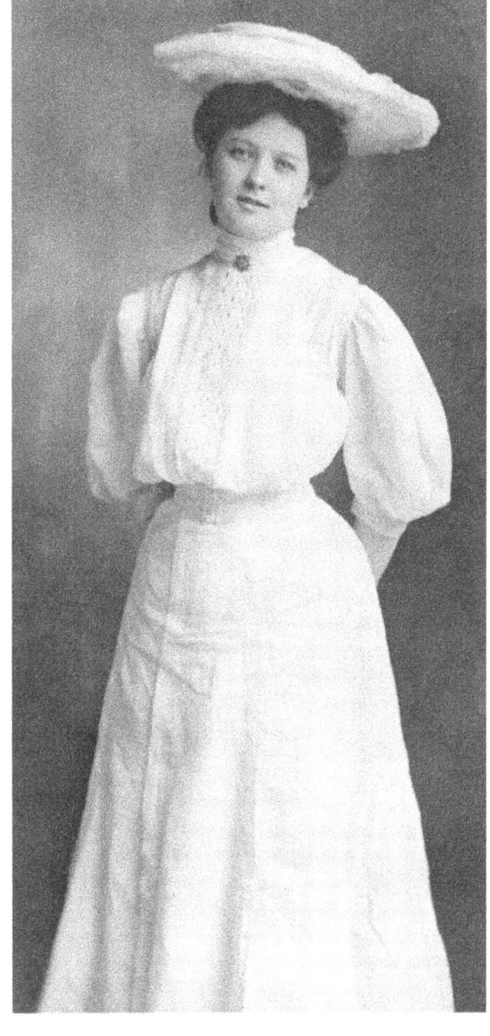

Edna at age seventeen when she worked as a clerk in a Milwaukee insurance office. *Deb Chester Maclin.*

and Armour, paved streets across Texas and built the Galveston Seawall after its 1900 hurricane.

Flora was no less busy in social and music circles and in what would become the Woman's Club of Fort Worth. As was typical of well-to-do women in the Progressive era, Flora interested herself in everything from hot lunches for students to the Industrial School for "wayward girls" north of Fort Worth. Daughter Florence was a mainstay in the social whirl of the young city and became a renowned singer.

Fort Worth, where Edna lived for nearly fifty years, began in 1849 as one of a string of military installations on the frontier of Texas. The army soon left, and the farmers and ranchers moved in, though most fled during the Civil War. The postwar cattle industry gave the town new life as the famous drives of so many western books and movies bestowed a new name on Fort Worth: Cowtown. Railroads brought even more wealth, and in impressive mansions above the Trinity River, the new elite now referred to their home as the Queen City of the Prairie. Its sixty thousand residents rushed headlong to create a full-blown modern city on what had been a few decades earlier only open land filled with deer and bison. The latest architecture and amenities

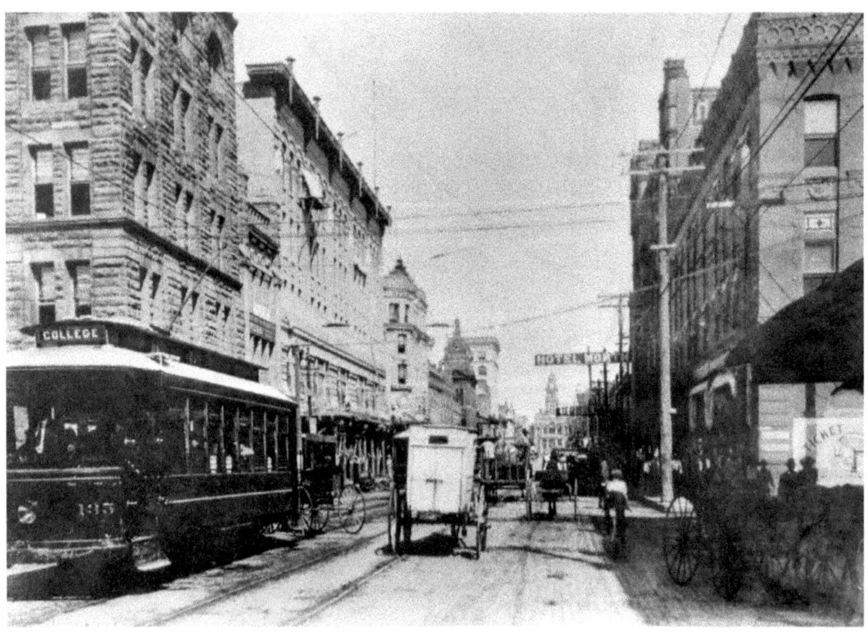

Downtown Fort Worth, circa 1904, when Edna arrived. *Genealogy, History and Archives Unit, Fort Worth Library, Historic Photographs Collection, A-0021.*

were embraced, from a natatorium to trolley cars to brick streets, which were disastrously slick in the rain. There were even sixteen automobiles and a Chinese restaurant when Edna arrived.

But in many ways, Fort Worth was still a small town where the movers and shakers all knew one another, did business with one another, lived near one another and partied together. The intricate web of social connections constructed by Arthur, Flora and Florence would quickly embrace Edna, too. This remarkable family took her in with open arms and unhesitatingly kept the secret of her birth. With her charming personality and the Goetzes to introduce her, Edna moved easily into a new society and forged her own network of friends and acquaintances who would ultimately help her save the institution that became her life's work.

Meeting Sam

But for now, Edna Kahly was an effervescent and attractive nineteen-year-old who burst onto Fort Worth's social scene like a firecracker. She and Florence, just a few months younger, were regulars in the society columns and on invitation lists. Despite the fear she must have harbored that someone would discover the secret of her birth, Edna's inner strength, already an integral part of her character, enabled her to appear vivacious and confident.

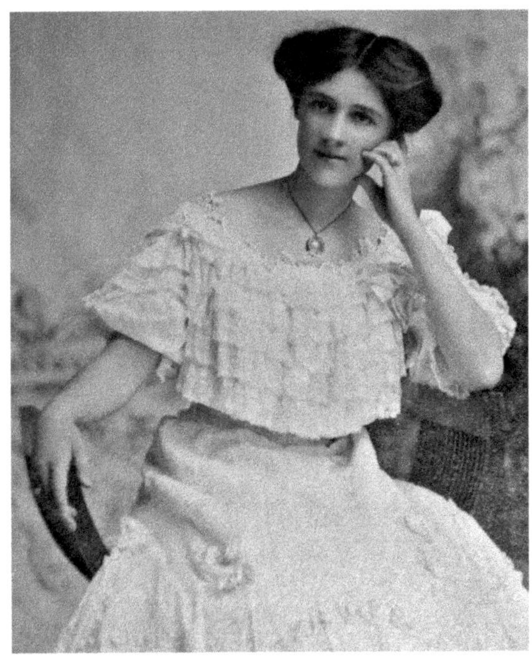

Florence Goetz, circa 1906. *Deb Chester Maclin.*

While still in Milwaukee, Edna had become attached to a handsome young Chicago man, Adolph Ehman, whose German-born family manufactured furniture. (He would figure in *Blossoms in the Dust* as her fiancé Damon, a play on

"Ehman.") He visited her in Fort Worth, but regrettably, only one letter from him has survived. Whether he knew of her birth is open to speculation, but they became engaged.

However, one tall, lanky Texas admirer did not let Adolph stand in the way of his attraction to Edna. Samuel William Gladney, born in 1877, grew up in Gainesville, on the Red River north of Fort Worth. More than six feet tall, he had blue eyes, wavy blonde hair and, according to Edna, "one of the most magnificent physiques" she had seen.

A bank cashier in Gainesville, Sam moved to Fort Worth in the summer of 1905 to work for his brother-in-law at Medlin (flour) Milling Company. When and where he met Edna is unknown, but it was likely at a May 1906 dance at a popular lakeside resort. Sometimes she claimed to have met the "impudent" Sam while cashing a check at a bank—a scene from *Blossoms*—and at other times she said only that they met when Sam worked for Medlin Mills.

He had little time to court Edna before she left to spend the summer of 1906 in Colorado Springs, Colorado. Since he couldn't plead his case in person, Sam besieged his beloved with letters and postcards as he traveled for Medlin across the South and to Cuba. He fussed about her health, told her of the sights and even tried to make her jealous by mentioning other girls. Mostly, he complained that she never wrote and, silently, worried about Adolph Ehman.

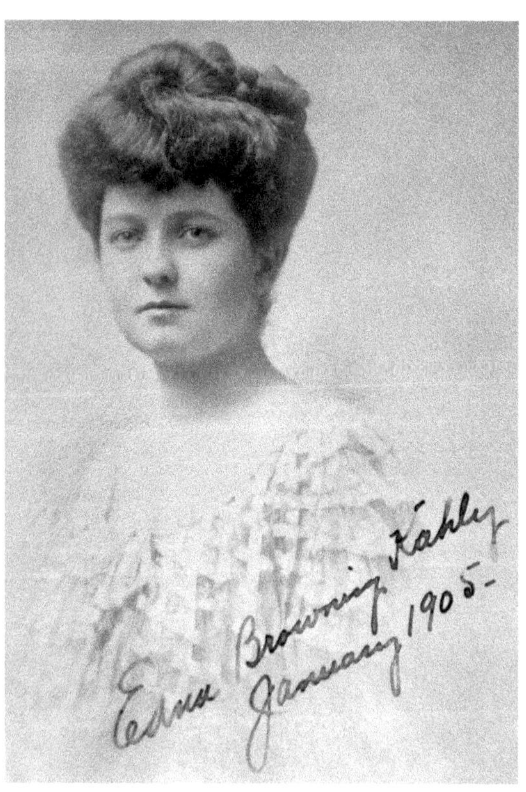

This portrait of Edna was used alongside one of Greer Garson in several *Blossoms in the Dust* press releases. *Deb Chester Maclin.*

Soon after Edna returned from Colorado to Fort Worth in September, Arthur and Flora Goetz announced that she would be married in their residence on Pennsylvania Avenue to Adolph. But two days before, she suddenly eloped to Gainesville—with Sam. The attraction, she later said, was that Sam was "unpredictable and loads of fun," loyal and true, a man to whom she had been able to confess her birth even while terrified that he wouldn't marry her because of it. Their love endured until his untimely death in 1935.

Learning About Edna

Sam soon learned that Edna "didn't know the word no. It wasn't in her vocabulary, and she always got what she wanted but did so in the nicest way."[5] Her drive was to help others despite Sam's hope that she would just be an "ordinary" wife and take care of him and their longed-for children. While they were courting, he had actively discouraged her from becoming a nurse, and though Sam may have thought he'd quashed the discussion, Edna had other ideas.

During a five-month sojourn in Cuba for Medlin Mills, she expressed a desire to visit a nearby leper hospital. Horrified, Sam refused to take her. As Edna retold the story to others over the years, she appeared to acquiesce but, in reality, took another tack. Very well, then, might she visit an old family friend who was a nun in the area? To that he agreed—only to discover that the friend worked in the San Lazaro Leper Hospital. Edna always laughed when she finished telling this story, saying, "I thought he'd never quit scrubbing himself after that visit."

Sam likely never tried again to control her charitable interests despite his fierce desire to shelter her from the sordid and seamy. He supported her in every way, even though he initially had little interest himself in saving the world. But Edna taught him to care. On their thirteenth wedding anniversary, he wrote, "My earnest hope is that...we shall be very happy and do much good for others in the years to come." But, he continued, "it almost makes me cry sometimes because God has not blessed us with any children."[6]

On one of their earlier Cuban trips, they had found to their delight that Edna had conceived. But joy was short-lived. Her pregnancy was an ectopic, or tubal, one where the woman's fertilized egg implants not in her uterus but in the fallopian tubes that carry the egg from the ovaries to the uterus. The egg cannot survive in that location. Today, if caught early enough, a tubal pregnancy does not have to mean a loss of the ability to conceive. But in Edna's day, the story was quite different, and death from blood loss was not uncommon.

One of the more poignant scenes in *Blossoms in the Dust* comes shortly after the death of Sam and Edna's fictional and only child. In it, Greer Garson as Edna cries that she feels cheated and useless, that she is no good for Sam and someone else would be better for him—and she means someone who could give him the child that she can't. They are words that resonate with every woman who's lost or been unable to conceive a child and must have come straight from Edna Gladney's heart as she told Ralph Wheelwright her story.

TAKING CARE OF EDNA

Sam's career in flour milling took the couple in 1909 to Wolfe City, north of Dallas, where he managed a plant for Medlin Mills. Edna worked part time in the office, using her old clerical skills from Milwaukee. She also became involved with Sam's employees, helping their wives with new babies and trying to interest them in healthier home lives.

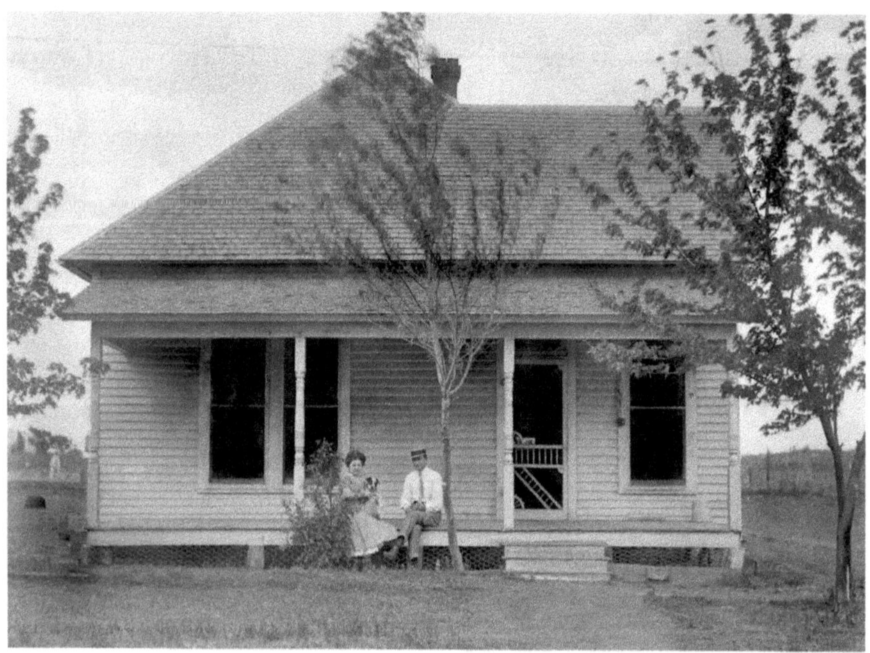

Edna, Sam and their dog Keeno on the porch of their Wolfe City home, circa 1912. *Deb Chester Maclin.*

Edna had her own health problems, though. From her mother's side of the family, she had inherited a tendency toward corpulence, which she spent the rest of her life fighting. Friends said that it was one of the few battles Edna ever lost. She made regular trips to drink the sulphur waters at health resorts, swam whenever she could and even visited "fat farms." Nowhere is her commitment to the fight more clearly illustrated than in this recipe for a "Reducing Mixture" found in one of her cookbooks: "1 large can of grapefruit juice, the juice of six lemons, two tablespoons of cream of tartar, and six tablespoons of Epsom salts. Mix well, drink before breakfast and at each meal if necessary." Despite this horrendous "cure," her weight fluctuated constantly and eventually led to diabetes.

In 1954, *Woman's Home Companion* noted that, even at sixty-six, Edna's "tremendous energy enabled her to do more in a day than 10 average people." Her cousin Mary Owen Routh, who lived and worked at the TCHAS from 1942 to 1946, agreed. "She had this tremendous drive and was always ready to go."

So it may have been the placidity of the Gladneys' life in Wolfe City that drove Edna to seek another outlet for her boundless vitality and benevolent interests. Exactly when and how she began her active relationship with the Texas Children's Home and Aid Society is unclear, but it likely was in 1911, when Reverend Morris established a ladies' auxiliary.

Finding Her Life's Work

Since Morris and his work on behalf of children were well known, Edna would have learned about the organization during the years she lived in Fort Worth before and after her marriage. An organization devoted to helping children would certainly have been of interest to Edna; there is some evidence that she served as the Home's volunteer liaison in the Wolfe City area.

But her real association began after the Gladneys moved to Sherman, Texas, northwest of Wolfe City, in 1913. With the financial backing of several prominent Texas millers, Sam bought a flour mill there and renamed it Gladney Milling Company. He soon began producing "Gladiola," a high-grade flour. Edna adopted the gladiola as her signature flower and filled their house on Crockett Street with bouquets.

Though Sam had once declared that he took little interest in politics, he did serve three terms on Sherman's city council. He quickly gained a

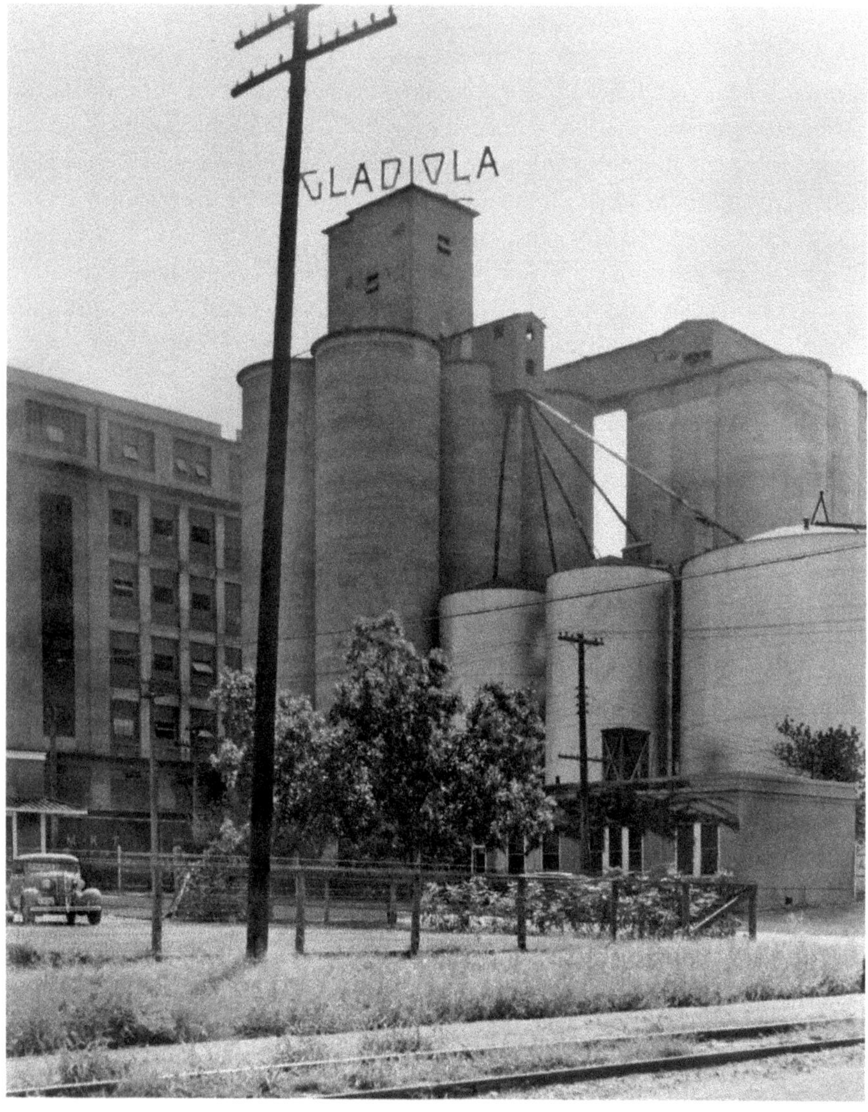

In 1913, Gladney Milling Company began making "Gladiola Flour," named for one of Edna's favorite flowers. *Deb Chester Maclin/Warner Bros. Entertainment.*

reputation as "honest, loyal, strict but fair and [with] the ability to make a man feel he was working with him rather than for him."[7] His civic service was good for business and also furthered his wife's charitable agenda as Edna quickly found several new causes.

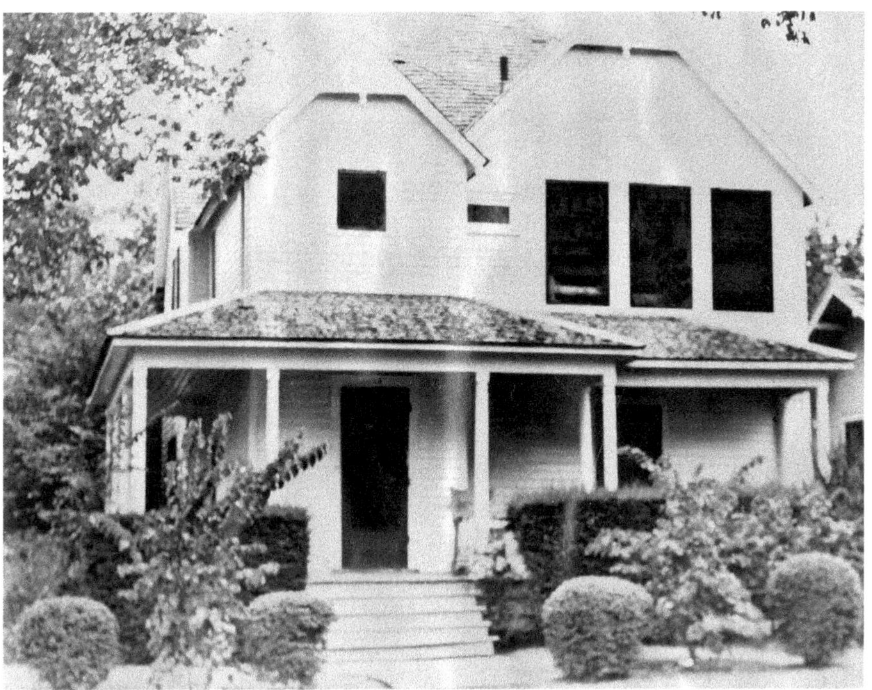

The first Sherman Day Nursery was located at 219 West Cherry Street and was probably the building depicted in *Blossoms in the Dust*. *University of California at Los Angeles/Special Collections.*

One of her first actions was to join the Sherman Civic League, organized "to cultivate higher ideals of civic life and beauty." (The members' pledge was more prosaic and included a promise not to spit on the floor in a streetcar, schoolhouse or other public building.) Composed mostly of women, the Sherman Civic League planted flowers, volunteered in schools, worked to control mosquito breeding grounds and prodded the city to hire a food inspector. Such activities were typical of America's Progressive era women, who had embraced new twentieth-century scientific concepts of life and work with unabashed enthusiasm. In Texas, the women used the power of their combined numbers to tackle gritty issues that affected hearth and home. And Texas men were often aghast to discover just how vast a sphere their wives and daughters considered that to be.

Edna began by inspecting public restrooms, checking on conditions at city grocers and meat markets and helping procure the city's first school health nurse. Then she discovered the Grayson County Poor Farm.

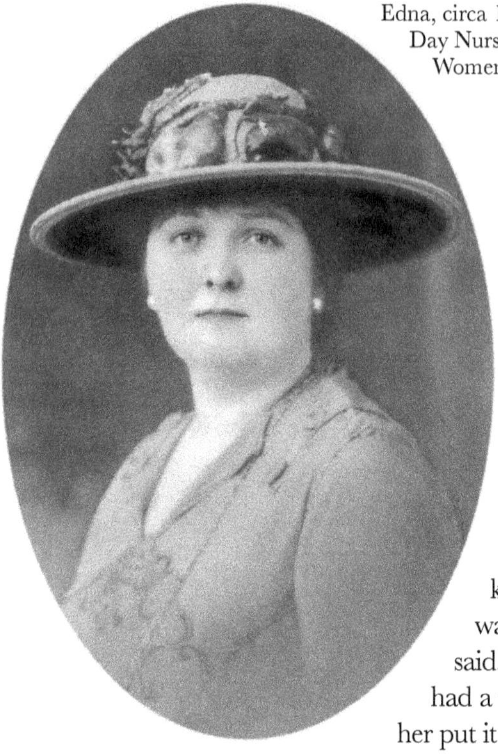

Edna, circa 1918, when she opened the Sherman Day Nursery and Kindergarten for Working Women. *Deb Chester Maclin.*

Poor farms were little more than dumping grounds for the poor, insane, transient, handicapped and even children. Edna was outraged at the conditions she found, particularly for the youngsters. The Sherman Civic League must do something, she declared. Friends shook their heads and knew she'd be calling them. "That was one thing about Edna," one said. "When she had an idea, she had a way of getting everybody to help her put it over." The speaker's wife agreed. "Yes, sir, and Edna's mind was an idea factory."[8]

She began the year 1917 by going on the attack with eight other socially prominent women from the Civic League. Edna wrote a newspaper article informing Sherman citizens that Grayson County Poor Farm children were filthy, uneducated and diseased. Sometimes several families occupied only a small room. One woman and her baby, both physically abused by the husband, had been living at the farm awaiting his trial. They were still there, declared an incensed Edna, while the husband had already been freed from jail.

Backed by her supporters, she carried her cause to Grayson County's governing body, the Commissioners Court. The *Sherman Courier* carried banner headlines and fifty-five column inches on the ensuing confrontation. The county health officer gently chided the ladies at the hearing: their object was commendable, but he was doing the best he could, and the newspaper had blown the problems out of proportion. Edna rose to her full height of five-foot-three and declared that "she herself had written [the article] and that it correctly set forth the conditions."

The health officer sat down and was not heard from again.

The county auditor jumped into the fray, saying there were a "hundred homes in Sherman where conditions were not as good as at the Farm." Edna rose once more. Yes, that was true, but they had to start somewhere. "These children [at the Poor Farm] are OUR children and it is OUR duty to properly care for them."[9]

Shortly after, the auditor, too, sat down and was not heard from again.

Undeterred by the county's lukewarm response, Edna marshaled her female troops and led them to the farm—whitewash, cleaning supplies and new mattresses in hand. The solution to the question of what to do with the children was obvious to Edna; she took them to Fort Worth and put them in the care of Belle Morris and the TCHAS.

Edna's now open relationship and volunteer duty with the Home exposed her to a whole new group in need: birth mothers, mostly single women facing society's scorn just as Minnie Jones had done. In her mother's honor, then, Edna became "mother confessor, legal counsel, nurse and temporary guardian of every girl within 40 miles of Sherman who needed confidential help."[10]

MGM screenwriter Ralph Wheelwright would expand on this history in his story idea for *Blossoms in the Dust* with a scene based on Edna's recollections. A young girl, he wrote, came to the Gladneys' residence one night, carrying a baby.

> *"You'll help me, won't you?" she pleaded. "Nobody knows I have this baby. They'd run me out of town." She pressed the tiny bit of life into Mrs. Gladney's arms. "Find a home for her, please. I don't want to have her live the kind of life I've had. Put her into the kind of home you'd like for your own child." The words remained long after the distressed girl vanished into the night.*

According to Wheelwright, Edna herself found a family for the infant:

> *Mrs. Gladney began writing letters to New York, Chicago, Fort Worth, Boston, Milwaukee, Detroit...She was keeping her pledge...The replies she received revealed that, besides the misfortunes of children without homes, there also existed saddened homes without children...Mrs. Gladney narrowed down her choice of homes, launched personal investigations and, finally, made the selection her conscience dictated.*

A Haven for Children

As World War I lengthened into its third and fourth years, another situation dealing with children came to Edna's attention. With thousands of American men away fighting in Europe—and no one knowing how much longer the conflict would last—women were hired to fill the positions they'd held in business and industries. This was particularly true in cities like Sherman, filled with flour mills and other manufacturing.

Edna saw the results every time she went to Gladney Milling. Children lived in shacks, played in filthy streets and were poorly clothed and fed. Many of their mothers could not afford to hire babysitters while they worked. The "idea factory" of her mind found a solution, one she had seen in Fort Worth: a day nursery to care for the children of working mothers.

She turned to the Civic League once more for support, receiving a promise of funds but also a request that she find other underwriting, too. Sam led the way as always, pledging generously. Edna found a large two-story house to rent just south of the courthouse and a few blocks west of the industrial district, a location that would attract female clerical, retail and manufacturing workers. She and her friends cleaned the grounds, prepared

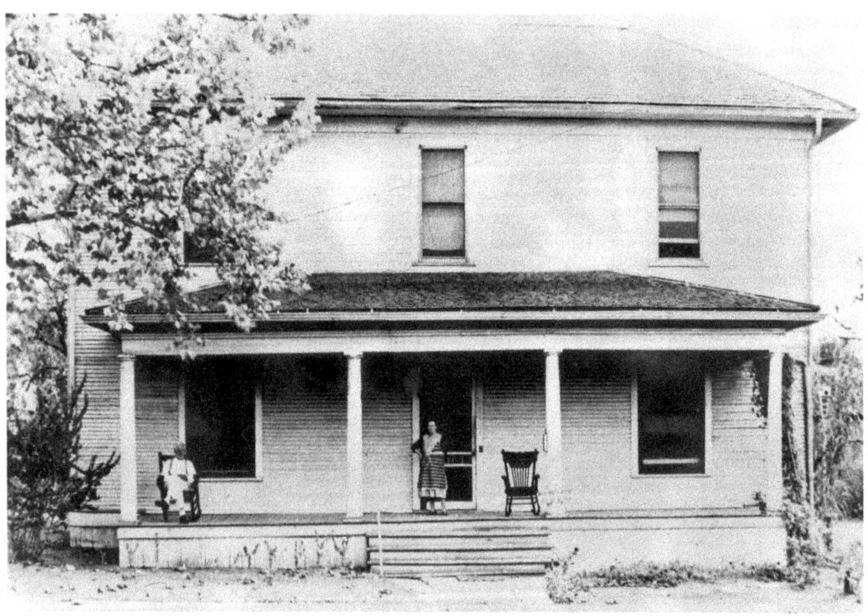

The second Day Nursery was at 314 East Cherry and had a large yard where the children could play. *University of California at Los Angeles/Special Collections.*

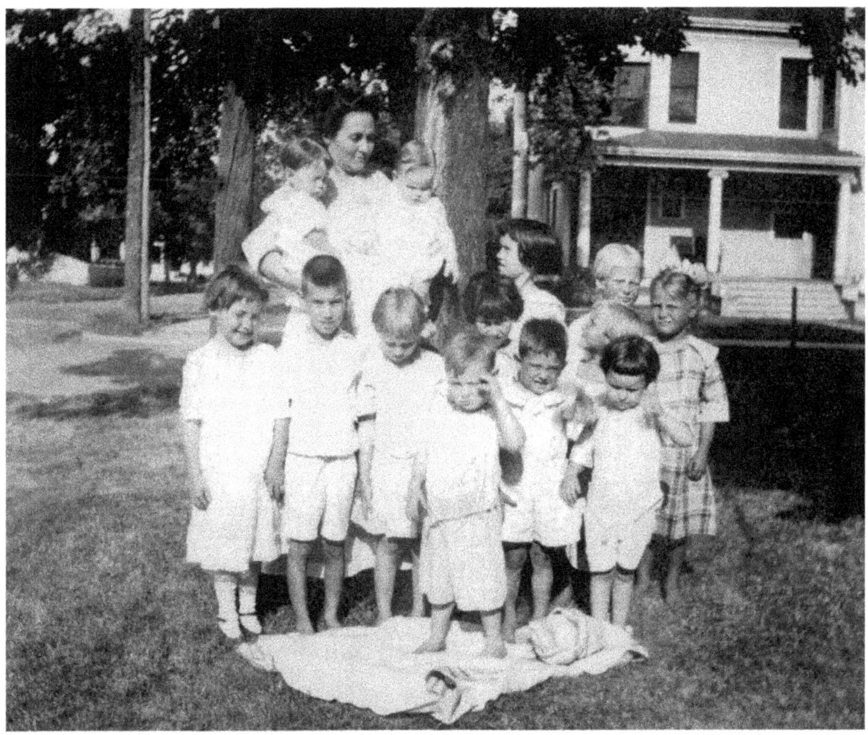

Day Nursery matron Mrs. Maggie Moore with some of the children who attended opening day on May 20, 1918. *Deb Chester Maclin.*

rooms and stained floors. Toys, dolls and a sand pile and swings outside provided entertainment and healthy physical exercise. The Sherman Day Nursery and Kindergarten for Working Women opened on May 20, 1918, with children and their mothers waiting at the door. The concept was an innovation in its day, and Sherman's was one of the very few such facilities in Texas.

Edna quickly realized that she needed more training. That summer, she traveled to New York City to study institutions similar to hers. Ralph Wheelwright wrote that she "studied settlement work in the slums, child welfare, public health, [and] parental education." Sam, at work in Sherman, wrote to his wife, "You are a fine girl and I am very proud of you."

On her return to Sherman, Edna put her new knowledge to work and continued her studies by auditing classes at North Texas Female College, not for credit "but only for my own satisfaction and information." Mary Routh recalled that her cousin was an avid reader and, like Thomas Jefferson, interested in all kinds of subjects. Because Edna had never finished high school, "everything," Mary said, "was a learning process for her. She was learning all the time and made time to read."[11]

Funding her day nursery was a constant chore. Drawing inspiration from Reverend I.Z.T. Morris, she placed large-mouthed glass milk bottles at soda fountains across town, staged musicals and then doggedly went door-to-door asking for donations. Years later, the facility would be taken over by the City of Sherman, which operated it until 2008, closing it ninety years after Edna founded it.

BACK TO FORT WORTH

For eight years, Sam and Edna led a comfortable lifestyle in Sherman that allowed them to build a new Prairie-style brick house, travel for pleasure—Edna particularly enjoyed her summertime escapes to cool Wisconsin—and help others.

But the cost was about to catch up with them.

One of Sam's first business moves had been to renovate the flour mill at an eventual price of several hundred thousand dollars and make it one of the most modern in the South. Spurred by World War I and huge new discoveries in Texas, oil had become an important "crop" in the state, and Sam invested there, too. He also bought real estate and, most disastrously, as it turned out, gambled on wheat futures. It was a tangled web of minimal returns, promissory notes and an unstable wheat market in the aftermath of the war. As Ralph Wheelwright would describe it in his *Blossoms* story idea, "Something suddenly happened to the world. Stock tickers jumped madly. In Chicago the bulls hammered the wheat pit." In the end, Sam's grain elevators were full of three-dollar-per-bushel wheat that had dropped to one dollar and wiped him out.

As that episode played out in *Blossoms*, Sam's request for a loan extension was denied by a Fort Worth mill because of the recent decline in the wheat market. His bookkeeper chided Sam for not declaring bankruptcy, predicting that he couldn't pay off all the debts in twenty years. In reality, Sam did pay some of them off within a few years but was still working at it when he died.

On April 11, 1921, Sam and Edna sold their new house with its furnishings and land and many of their personal possessions to two Texas flour millers who had been friends and backers for years. Almost the entire sale price went

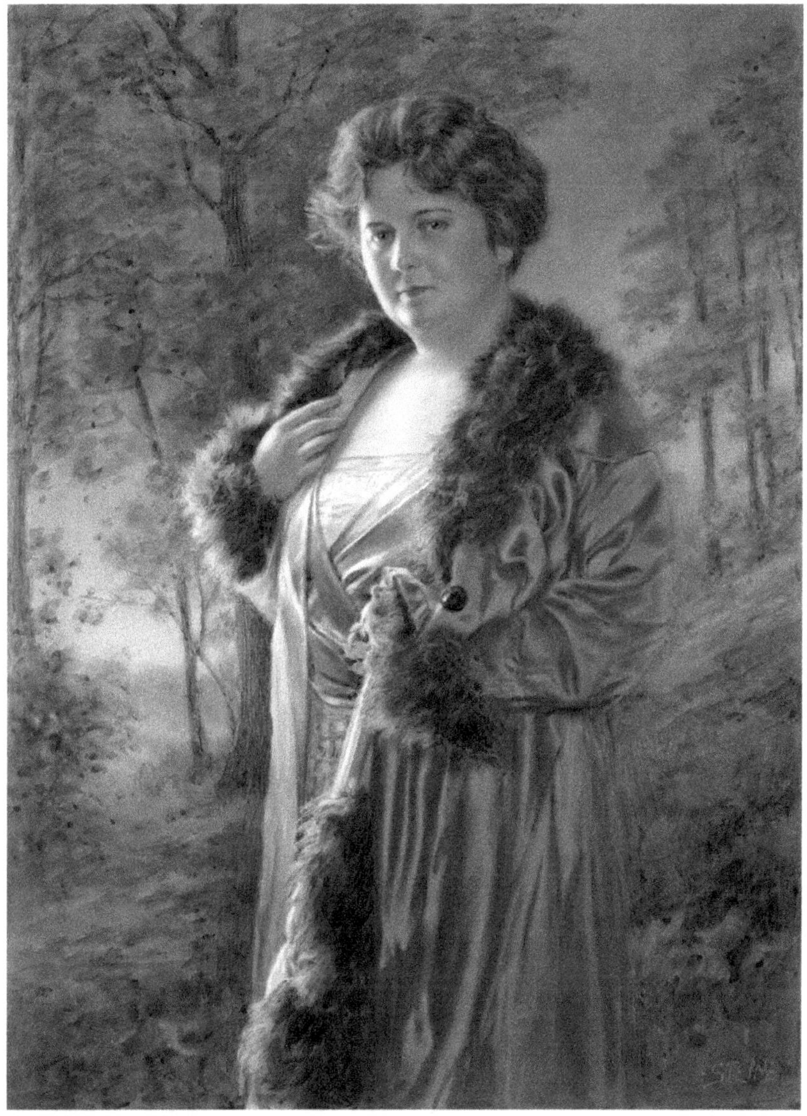

This 1921 portrait by Julian Stein, one of Milwaukee's top photographers, was made on a visit home. *Deb Chester Maclin.*

to debt payment, but it was only the beginning of long years of struggle. Sam's mill was sold and became Fant Milling Company, which continued to produce his Gladiola Flour. The women of the Tuesday Literary Club took over operation of Edna's day nursery for several years. And on one of her final days there, Edna went around town for the last time to collect coins from the milk bottles. "Virtually everybody in Sherman wept," reported the *Sherman Democrat.* The paper took the unusual step of saluting the Gladneys' and their efforts on the city's behalf. "Fort Worth is to be congratulated on securing them for residents of that city."[12]

Left with little but their clothes and two automobiles, Sam and Edna headed "home" to Fort Worth, even as aviators were dropping pamphlets on that city about the dire financial need of the Texas Children's Home and Aid Society.

Chapter 3

THE HEART OF A CRUSADER

"We drove to Fort Worth to make a fresh start," Edna later said. "Fort Worth offered opportunity." For a time, the couple lived with family or friends while Sam worked to repay debts.[13] A flour milling associate offered him a position with Fort Worth Elevators Company, which exported and imported grain.

Edna took art history and sociology classes at Texas Christian University, joined the board of the Fort Worth Welfare Association—whose chairman for years was her uncle, Arthur Goetz—and indulged her fascination for the offbeat by undergoing a psychological analysis to help her choose a vocation. It showed strengths she would soon bring into play: abstract comprehension, good reaction time, concentration, a natural executive capacity, diplomacy and sympathy. It also showed her dislike of monotonous details and an imagination that measured one hundred—the top of the scale.

In the fall of 1922, Edna used those qualities when she captained a team to raise money for the TCHAS's proposed new receiving facility. Though the short two-month campaign secured little more than half of its goal, Edna's group had the second-highest total overall and the highest in her division. So it's no surprise that, three months later, this canny fundraiser was elected not only to the board of directors but also as secretary of the executive committee.

Financially, the Gladneys' lives began to improve. In July 1923, Sam left Fort Worth Elevators to establish, with a partner, the wholesale Gladney-Muchmore Grain Company; Edna worked in the office. *Blossoms in the Dust*

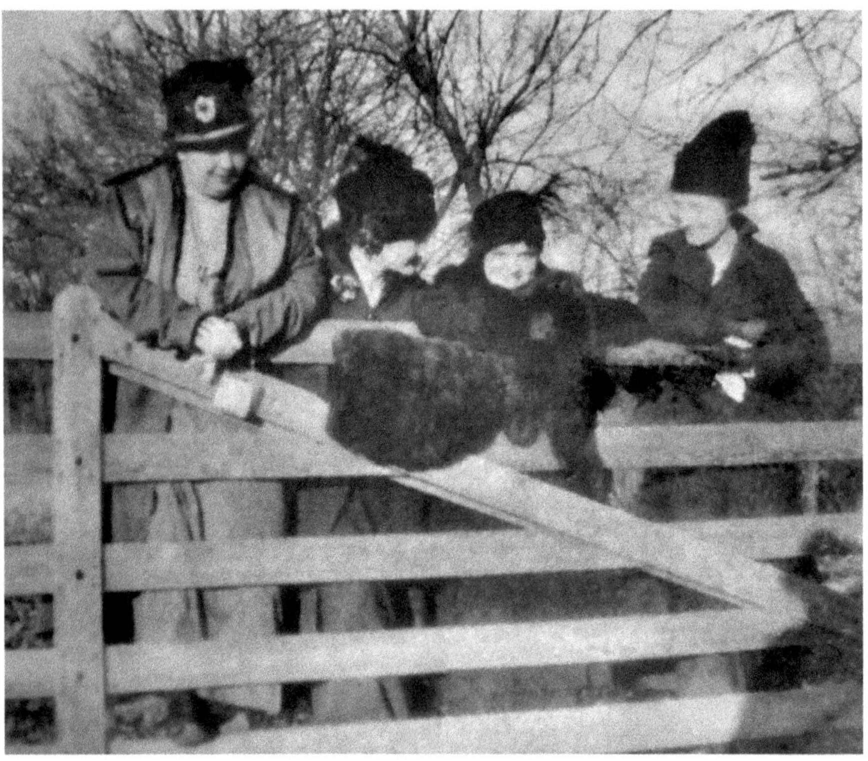

Edna (on the left) enjoyed trips home to Milwaukee to see family and friends. *Deb Chester Maclin.*

is a bit vague about this period, depicting a nameless mill with Sam working in the foreman's office—which he calls "*the company's* private office." He has developed the "Gladney Wheat Wastage Process" and wishes to patent it, but no documentation has been found that such a patent actually existed.

Sam felt comfortable enough by this time to think about having a house of their own again, so Edna contacted her cousin, architect Frank Lloyd Wright, to design it. Already famous, Wright (1867–1959) no longer did many smaller houses but made an exception for Edna since they were related through Minnie Kahly's family. His design, which still survives in the Wright archives, was meant to be built on a steeply sloping lot in the Forest Park section of Fort Worth, overlooking the Trinity River and the zoo, and was one of the earliest examples of his distinctive cantilever style.

But before construction could start, it was halted by new money woes. Two years after starting his own business, Sam dissolved that partnership and launched Gladney Grain Company with himself, Edna and his brother Jim Gladney as incorporators. He may also have had a silent partner, flour miller Kay Kimbell, whom he and Edna knew from their Sherman days.

No records from either company have survived except for one telegram from Kimbell to Sam in September 1926, telling him of a grievous error in the company books but assuring him that the capital was no more than half lost. "We can keep the business going and regain this small loss and get the business back on a paying basis." Sam took out the cash value of his insurance policies to help stay afloat but could not pay back a note he owed to Bert K. Smith, head of Smith Bros. Grain Company. In late 1929, that debt led to a lawsuit with Smith that dragged on for years and eventually resulted, after Sam's death, in his defeat.

At the Texas Children's Home, Belle Morris died in 1924, and Roy Stockwell left the following year to take a similar position in Georgia. Two consecutive short-term superintendents, Ethel Webber and Lillie Wilson, tried to continue plans for the new receiving facility; Edna was among the board members still working on the project. She also visited the private houses where TCHAS boarded the infants and youngsters in their care. She may have been volunteering to help with the children, too. Several letters to her from Sam mention babies "who miss you" and update her on several more whose health has improved.

In addition, Edna joined the Girls' Protective Association, formed during World War I, which helped "girls from the streets, girls who have been released from jails, and young unmarried mothers," some of them reduced to living in hovels with "wagon sheet roofs and no floors."[14]

Ringing Doorbells

By 1927, the Texas Children's Home was more than $7,000 in debt (about $100,000 today) and owned no property of any kind; it had an office in the Cotton Exchange Building, and children were kept at private boardinghouses across the city. And despite the absence of records—many of the Home's early files were lost in a fire or later discarded—it's probable that the organization was on the verge of closing after nearly four decades.

In *Blossoms in the Dust*, the TCHAS had not yet entered the picture. Instead, Edna happens upon adoption hearings at the Tarrant County Courthouse, where orphans from a state institution are being legally placed with new parents. Edna is appalled to find them tagged like cattle and to see an illegitimate infant spurned by prospective parents from a "conservative neighborhood" who fear ostracism because of baby Tony's "bad blood." The eugenics movement of the early twentieth century stressed purity of bloodline to achieve the best possible human being, a concept that enjoyed some popularity in social work. So even though Tony's mother is of a good family, her status as an unwed mother negates that, while his unknown father is even more suspect. In this scene, the judge gives both Tony and a young boy to Edna if she can place them each in a home within two weeks.

That was Hollywood's version of how Edna began placing children. In reality, and as a last-ditch effort to save the TCHAS, the board of directors turned to her as a proven fundraiser who loved children and had experience with unwed mothers. They asked Edna to take the position of superintendent but could not afford to pay her a salary.

Edna must have been torn by competing needs. This was the work she'd been born to do, yet she and Sam were experiencing financial difficulties; prudence dictated that she find a paying job or at least continue helping in the Gladney Grain office so a clerk needn't be hired. Though Sam was compassionate and supportive, he urged her not to accept, probably fearing that the job was beyond anybody. They finally compromised: she would work for six months to get funds and records in order—no more.

In April 1927, Edna began her six-month term—one that lasted until her death in 1961 and required her to work at no salary for the first several years.

The job was prodigious, and deciding where to start must have been daunting: even placements had been handled poorly, and many children were "with quite mediocre families."[15] She once more resurrected Reverend I.Z.T. Morris's glass milk bottle banks and, according to Ralph Wheelwright, wrote letters and went door-to-door as she had done in Sherman, soliciting donations and raising about $7,000. (Some ads for *Blossoms in the Dust* blared, "She rang every doorbell in Texas!" above artwork of a dainty gloved hand ringing a bell.) But, Ralph continued, unpaid board bills and medical expenses for the children quickly ate through the money.

Finding a Home

Equally as important as funds was a building to bring all the children together under one roof. For that, Edna turned to newspaperman, businessman and

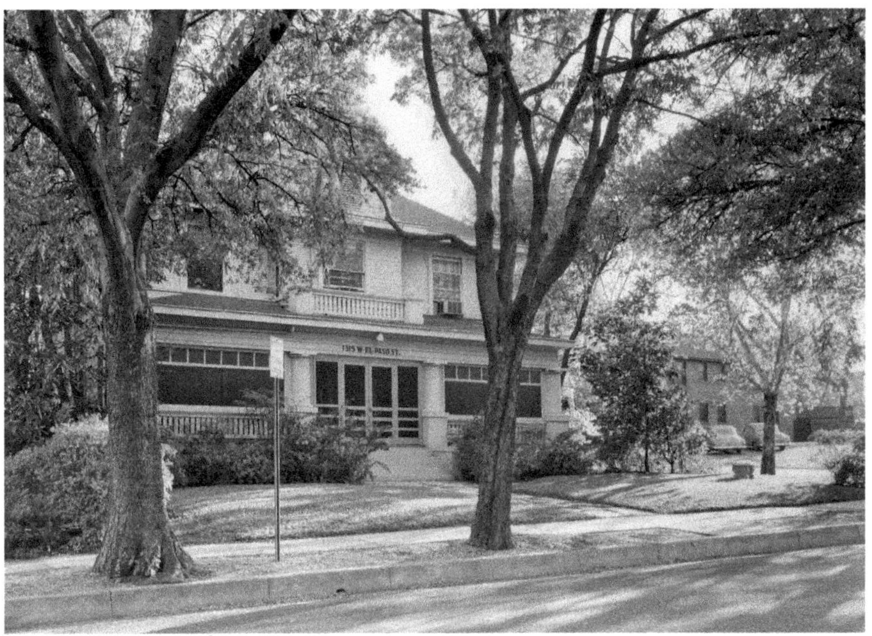

The Baby Home at 1315 West El Paso Street was razed after Edna's death. *Deb Chester Maclin.*

Fort Worth promoter Amon G. Carter (1879–1955). He and Arthur Goetz belonged to many of the same organizations and served on committees together, giving Edna an entrée to him. Carter, wrote Ralph Wheelwright, told her to find a building and he'd get it for her.

She located a large, two-story Colonial Revival house on El Paso Street, a genuine home, not an institution. Carter's efforts to purchase it eventually led him to A.J. Duncan (1878–1955), who had arrived in the city only a year or so after him to manage an electric power company. This nephew of U.S. president William McKinley had soon bought out or merged his company with nearly all his competitors; today, his one-time Texas Power and Light Company is TU Electric.

Duncan, who was also on the board of First National Bank, negotiated the purchase of the house at 1315 West El Paso in August 1929 from cattleman John R. Halsell. The buyer, technically, was the First National Company, which was affiliated with the bank. The Halsells had already moved, and the Fort Worth City Directory shows the TCHAS occupying the house in early 1929. Duncan provided the property rent-free until 1950, when he conveyed it outright as a gift.

Blossoms in the Dust shows Edna first using a storefront for rent; a sign proclaims it to be the Texas Children's Home & Aid Society—the first time that title is used in the film (and one of the reasons so many people think she established it). But city government shuts down the operation as a violation of zoning laws. Deeply discouraged, Edna returns home to find that Sam is ill. He has sold the rights to his wheat wastage process and gives her the check for her children.

She declares that she's through with the babies, but Sam knows her too well. Before dying in her arms, he urges her to "fight for those kiddies of yours if you have to ring every doorbell in Texas." A montage follows, depicting a black-garbed Edna receiving money in her ever-present glass milk bottle from all types and races of people across Texas.[16] With the money, the screen Edna acquires the El Paso Street house, accurately rebuilt on the MGM lot down to the screened porches and the spindles in the staircase. Even the pink bassinet familiar to many hundreds of real adoptive parents is there. Made for the birth of Dorothy Kahly Dumas's daughter Edna Jane in 1926, it was later moved to the Baby Home for presenting babies to new parents and is still a treasured family heirloom.[17] Amon G. Carter's role in acquiring the building was to have been shown in *Blossoms*, but he declined to be represented.

By 1929, then, Edna had accomplished in less than two years what had been needed for nearly three decades. But acquiring what she later described as "this lovely Love Nest" was only the first step.

MAKING HOMES

Ralph Wheelwright portrayed this moment of realization in his story idea for *Blossoms in the Dust*. "All was well until time to move in. Mrs. Gladney made the discovery that she was without sufficient equipment or furniture. She slumped in the middle of the great, bare house and wept."[18] Sam, though struggling to pay debts, borrowed on his insurance policies to help while Edna ransacked thrift stores and begged friends for furniture. She could afford or find only a few baby beds, so the smallest infants, who could not yet turn over, slept in baskets. These early struggles are not depicted in *Blossoms*.

Older children slept in other parts of the house, and little is known about them: Edna rarely made their photographs public since they could be identified more easily than the babies. All ages enjoyed the screened porches that made summer sleeping easier and the expansive backyard, which Edna began to transform with lush flower beds, trees and a brick sidewalk for taking perambulators full of babies on their daily outings.

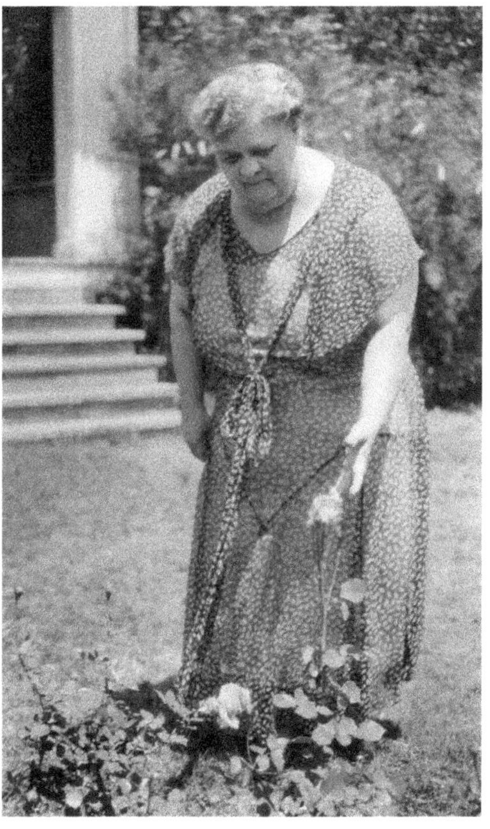

Edna's mother, Minnie Kahly, lived at and managed the Baby Home from 1930 until her death in 1938. *Deb Chester Maclin.*

Soon there was a real mother to oversee it. Minnie Jones Kahly moved from Milwaukee to Fort Worth in 1930 to live in and manage the Baby Home, leaving Edna free for administration and fundraising. Minnie, a beloved figure, stayed on the job until her death in 1938.

One of Edna's most important duties was selecting families in which to place children. Amazingly, an account of her very first placement as superintendent of the TCHAS exists in some very brief notes she jotted down in 1947, with the apparent idea of writing a book. (She was regularly asked to write about her work but never had time.)

The child to be adopted was a boy of "Dutch Indian" and American blood whom she placed in a small, unnamed West Texas oil town. Taking him there herself on the train, she turned him over to the new parents, who "received him with all the love and welcome in the world." When night fell, the happy family took her to a hotel so new it was still unpainted. The owner/manager, a very large and commanding woman, told them she didn't take in "ladies," apparently not caring to cater to the "ladies of the night" popular in oil field towns. The new parents promptly reassured her. "Well, she [Edna] ain't no lady, she's a nurse and brought our baby, and you better take care of her."

"Which she did," Edna wrote, talking for hours about her own children and "how hard she had worked to keep them together and in school."

The boy Edna placed, she noted with satisfaction, later graduated from high school, served in World War II and married. He "knows he has the finest father and mother in the world and [is] starting out in life well equipped to make a useful citizen," she wrote.

Her method for choosing parents was well explained in *Blossoms* in a scene where Edna gives a child to new adoptive parents. She spent weeks, even months, studying both prospective parents and the child, believing that they "should love the same things and, as far as possible, have the same characteristics." This was the social work practice known as matching that had recently become popular and would remain so until the 1970s. In adoptions where the parents and child were not biologically related, it was an attempt to mimic "natural" families, who share physical, social and racial characteristics. Even mental capacity was taken into consideration, a process that new tests made easier.

In one area, though, Edna differed radically from accepted practice. She believed in placing a baby as early as possible rather than waiting for six or eight months, even a year or more, to see how the child turned out physically and mentally. A home and a family and love were much more important to pediatric development, in her opinion.

But seeing the child leave was an emotional upheaval for her. "I work like fury to get them adopted, then cry like a fool when they go," she declares in *Blossoms*. The "real" Edna sometimes added, "The Mississippi River was behind my eyes, waiting to spill over."

Sentimental Edna may have been, but anyone who mistook that for weakness rarely made the same mistake twice.

"It Was Do or Die with Her"

By the early 1930s, Edna had transformed the Texas Children's Home and had a staff, including her mother, on whom she could depend. Now—at last—she could embrace the challenge she'd longed to fight for years.

Adoption was still very much "a hush-hush matter; an adopted child was suspect [and] often pitied."[19] Many prospective parents refused to even consider a child born out of wedlock for fear that the illicit nature of his birth would result in character flaws and health defects. The eugenics movement was driving a new theory in social work, exemplified in a pamphlet entitled *The Degenerate Children of Feeble-Minded Women.*[20] Unwed mothers were

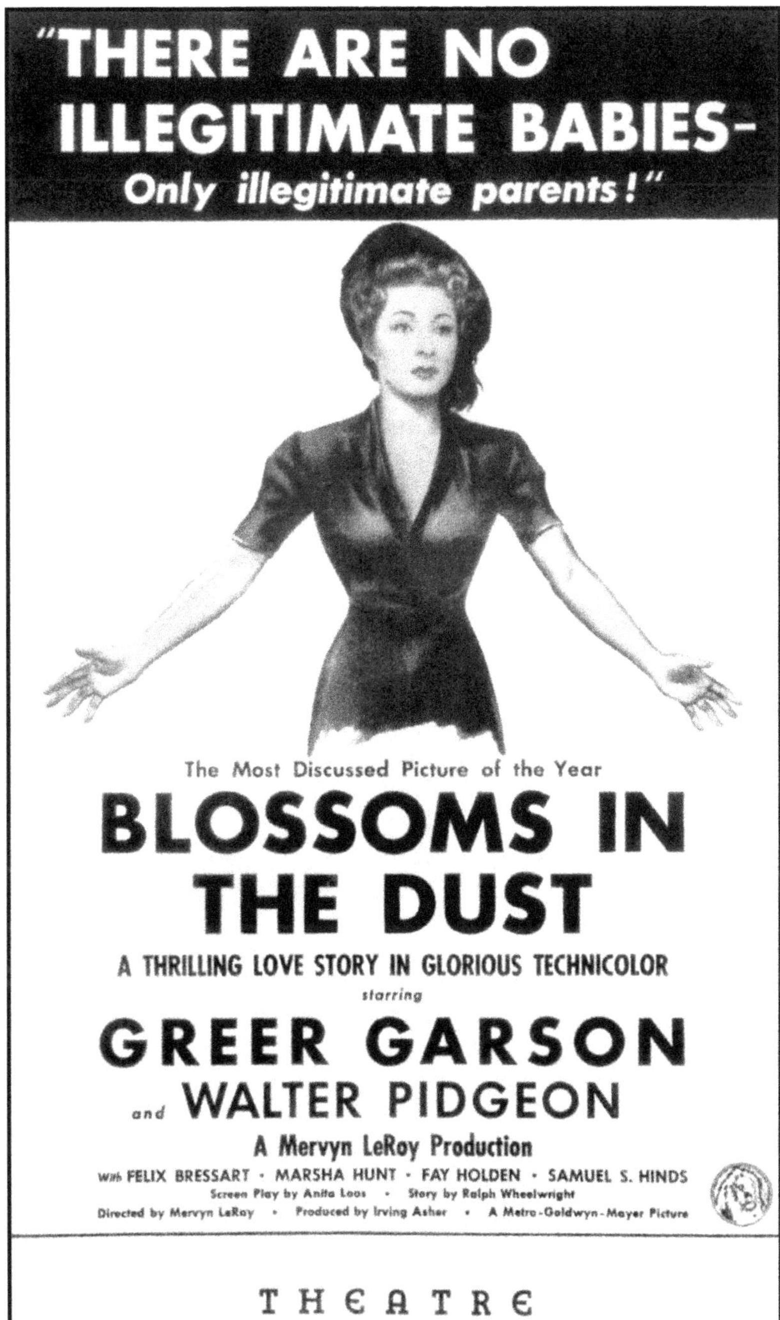

This theater lobby poster was designed by MGM's publicity department. *Deb Chester Maclin.*

"oversexed" and "subnormal" and would therefore produce unfit babies. Many states were actually sterilizing such women to "check the increase" of mental illness and to lessen crime.

And a child had no way to obscure such a heritage since birth certificates issued across the country for out-of-wedlock babies were boldly stamped "illegitimate."[21]

Edna knew their pain intimately.

As early as 1930, Texas newspapers began quoting what became, thanks to *Blossoms in the Dust*, her most famous catchphrase: "There are no illegitimate children, only illegitimate parents."[22] As the "reel" Edna exclaimed to Dr. Breslar, she hated "the injustice of branding innocent little nameless children in records where everyone can see…it is cruelty, inhuman cruelty." In the film, she has an epiphany: "I know my cause [now] and it's as clear as daylight. Every human being…deserves the right to make its own name without bigotry or prejudice…I'm going to fight for that right."

In reality, Edna had known that cause all her life. As her cousin Mary Owen Routh said, "She was driven to it. It was do or die. She could have walked away [from the hurt] but she jumped in with both feet to help those children."[23] After *Blossoms in the Dust* came out, so many people wrote Edna about birth records that she resorted to a form letter. "For longer than I like to remember," she wrote bluntly, "bigotry, with its own brand of stupidity and cruelty, was dictator of the destiny of thousands of so-called 'illegitimate' children in Texas. I shan't allow myself to even recite in this letter the unbelievable injustices which have been inflicted upon and committed against such children."

MAKING A LAW

During Texas's Mexican period (1821–36), the law considered all children whose births were not registered by their mothers to be illegitimate. Not until 1868 was that law amended by the then state of Texas, requiring *both* parents to register the birth. The onus to do so remained on them until 1903, when registration duty was moved to the attending physician or midwife, but there was little, if any, follow-up. Nor was Texas the only state to be so lax. In 1912, the *El Paso Herald* noted that only a handful had such modern laws, and their reports were often incomplete. In no other civilized nation, chided the *Herald*, was there such a neglect of vital statistics.[24] Registration was needed to enforce child labor and compulsory education laws, settle estates and provide medical help to those in need.

World War I brought a partial end to the shilly-shallying: enlistment in the military had required a birth certificate since 1909. The Texas legislature created a Bureau of Vital Statistics in 1917, but county response to registrations continued to be lackadaisical. In 1929, the certificates still required that the baby be designated as legitimate or illegitimate, but state legislators refused to allow the name or "any other identifying information" about the "illegitimate" father to be included. (As late as 1975, this was still the law.)

About this time, Texas social workers and "a very small number of socially minded people," as Edna wrote, began the long campaign to remove "illegitimate" from state birth certificates as these documents had been modified in several bills in the 1920s and early 1930s. They targeted the records of adopted children, noting that "there is now no law providing for the issuing of birth certificates of adopted children under their adopted [as opposed to their birth] names." Texas House Bill 732, passed in 1935, removed the offensive word but, Edna fumed, left "adopted mother" and "adopted father" on the form. The natural assumption of readers would be that, if the child was adopted, he or she was therefore probably born out of wedlock.

Even some adoptive parents disagreed with her stance, while many others accused her of aiding immorality. The law bounced in and out of the legislature for several years as lawmakers fixed one portion only to disrupt another. "For a long time," Edna wrote in her form letter, "our legislators could not see the problem at all."

Blossoms depicted this in several scenes. One supportive Texas legislator tells her she's opening up "a hornet's nest," another says that the bill would be "a direct blow at the sanctity of the home" and yet a third declares that "you can't override the prejudice of centuries." Soon after, three matrons ask her "to stop this long fight for immoral legislation...because it encourages the young to be bad." They realize she believes she's doing good, but "nice people have to be segregated from those who are evil." In response, Edna asks them to pick out the three illegitimate children from the dozen playing in the yard. Of course, they cannot.

The climactic scene in *Blossoms* is the one played out in the west gallery of the Texas Senate when Edna rises to forcibly address legislators. (Some movie critics later wrote that Greer Garson should have won the Academy Award for this scene alone.) But the real Edna Gladney was not, in her own words, "an exhibitionist," and she never made such a speech.

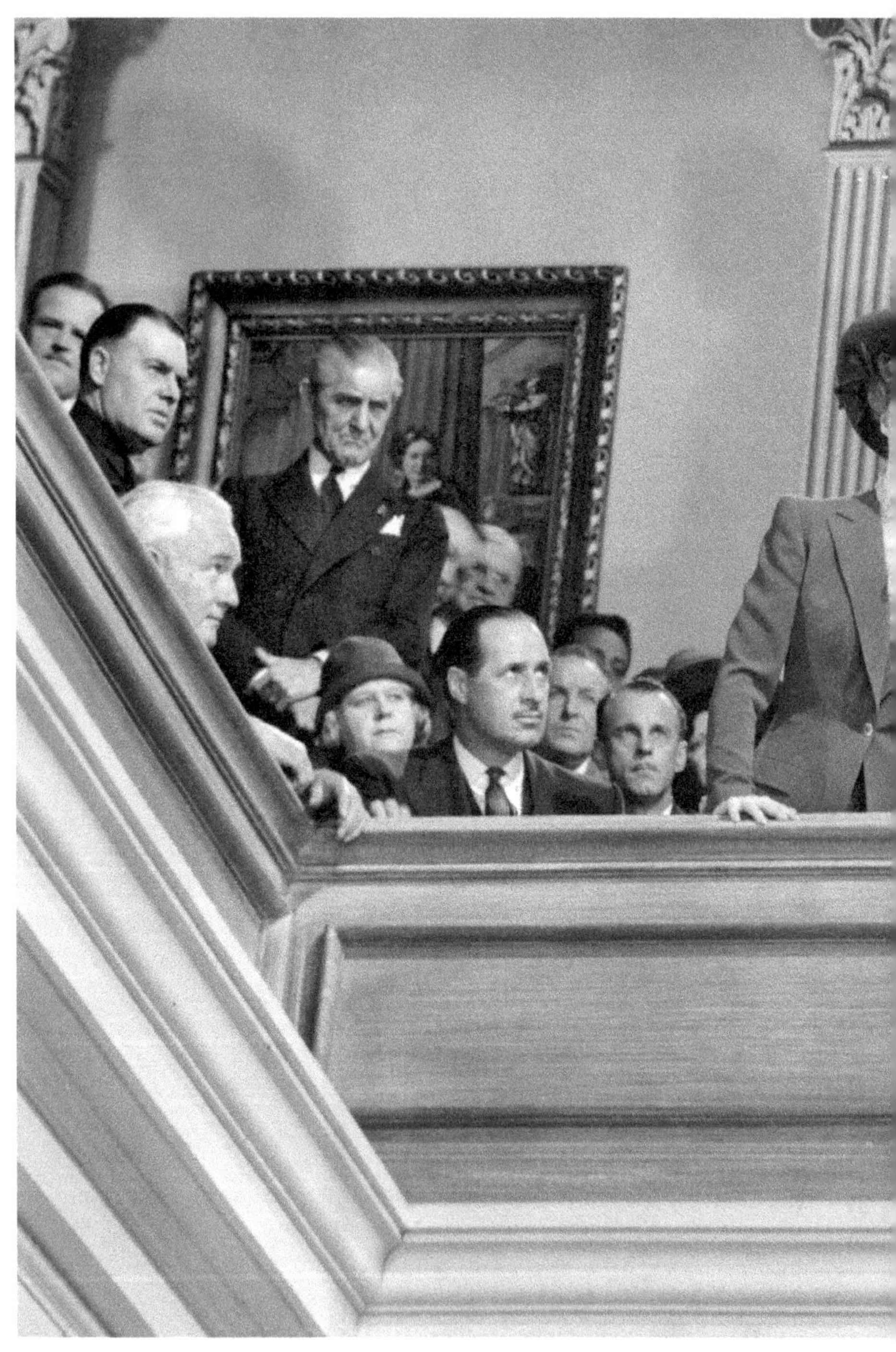

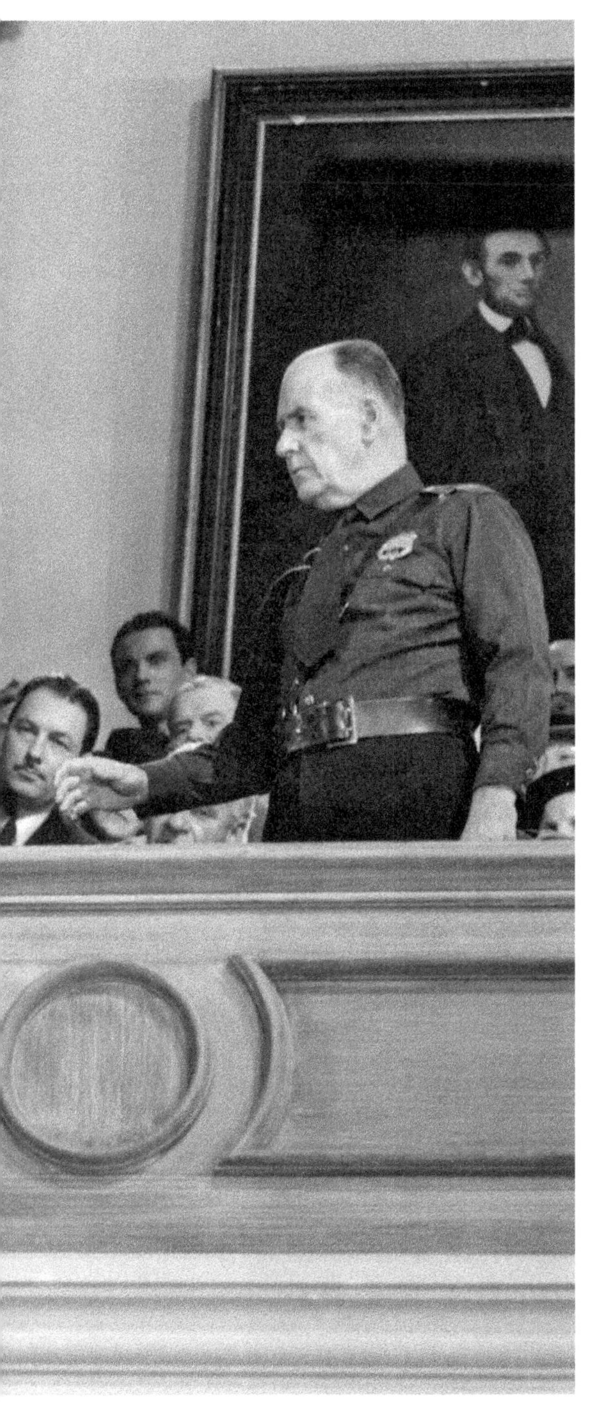

Her work, and that of TCHAS board members and lawyers, was done behind the scenes, gathering data from other states, educating social and civic leaders, drafting bill models, enlisting doctors and medical organizations and presenting information to the public, as Edna wrote to Ralph Wheelwright. According to her, Home attorney Cecil Hubbert made many trips to Austin "solely to explain to the Bureau [of Vital Statistics] how the law must be worded in order not to defeat its purpose. But even after this, the Bureau and various legislators who became interested in the law, failed to incorporate certain important features of the form of the new certificate. So, again, Mr. Hubbert returned to Austin to repeat [the Texas State Conference of Social Welfare's] request more forcibly and in more detail."[25]

Greer Garson as Edna speaks to the Texas legislature. *The Gladney Center for Adoption.*

"There were various objections," Edna continued, "which had to be overcome and have since proven ill-founded, and which had to be attacked in a rather indirect manner, which we pursued in this office while Mr. Hubbert visited our four District Judges here, one by one, explained the cooperation that we needed...and thus obtained from them their direct correspondence with the Bureau of Vital Statistics and with the Attorney General's Office."

Edna's work took her across Texas, so she knew the judges and doctors she needed to convince. Her efforts and the Home's were not in the public record, she said, and she graciously gave credit to Addilee Abell of Wichita Falls for pushing the legislation through.[26] MGM, she later wrote, knew the facts and chose to "fictionize" those scenes for dramatic value.[27]

Today, some advocates of open adoption records believe that this birth certificate law was the beginning of Edna's drive to close birth and adoption records to adoptees, as they still are in many states. One website (www.netaxs.com) claims that she did this to encourage people to adopt so that she might build a chain of maternity homes and become "the largest baby broker" in the country. The author of the site has confused Edna with Georgia Tann, the infamous "baby thief" who ran the Tennessee Children's Home Society. (Oddly, though, Tann worked briefly at the Texas Home in 1920 as a college student.) The fact is that most of the restrictive legislation was passed years after Edna Gladney's death. She herself always urged her parents to tell their children they were adopted and worked to obtain as complete a medical history of the birth parents as was possible, in case it was needed in the future.

Losing Her Heart

But Edna was unable to celebrate when HB 732 passed that May. In the midst of her campaigning efforts for it, Sam Gladney died in her arms on Valentine's Day 1935.

On February 12, he had suffered a heart attack at his Universal Mills office, where his successful career as sales manager began in 1931; his condition was not thought to be critical. His funeral on February 15 was held in the expansive Mediterranean-style house the Gladneys had rented on Medford Court, near where they had planned to build Frank Lloyd

Wright's house. Among the pallbearers were Universal Mills owner Gaylord Stone and longtime friend Kay Kimbell, who established his Kimbell Art Foundation later that same year. (It and his collection became the basis of the internationally known Kimbell Art Museum, which opened in 1972.)

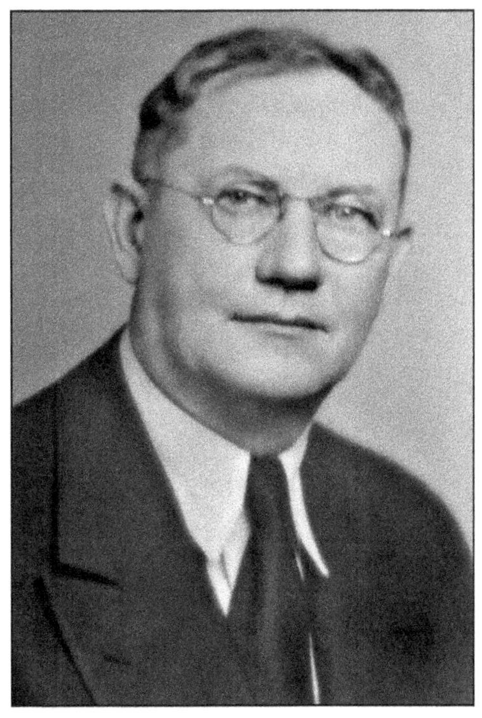

Edna cherished a telegram from Walter Pidgeon, telling her it was a "privilege to have played so fine a role as that of Samuel Gladney," pictured here in 1934. *Deb Chester Maclin.*

Fort Worth attorney Charles Kassel, a childhood friend of Sam's from Gainesville, guided Edna through the probate process. Sam left only $4,600 (about $78,000 today) in personal property, his insurance policies and several notes that were owed him—all else had gone to pay off his debts from Sherman, the court costs of his long case against Bert K. Smith and generous gifts he made to help keep the Texas Children's Home afloat.

Chapter 4

HOLLYWOOD COMES CALLING

Sam's death left Edna so shaken and lost that she determined to leave her position at the Texas Children's Home where there were so many memories of him. Testaments to her dispirited mind are the photos she had taken of the interior of the Medford Court house she would soon have to vacate; a framed portrait of Sam is in almost every one as is Edna. There's no doubt that her mother, Minnie Kahly, helped her deal with her grief. Another supporter was Reverend Lee Heaton, pastor of Trinity Episcopal Church, whom she often credited with helping her return to life.[28]

Money problems exacerbated her situation. A year after Sam's death, and at the suggestion of her attorney, Edna wrote to Gaylord Stone at Universal Mills to ask if any of Sam's bonus money was left. She had lived "a thousand years" since Valentine's Day 1935, she told Stone, and been forced to borrow money to live on while the estate was settled. With Sam gone, she had chosen to dedicate herself to unwanted children and enclosed a brochure on the Home so Stone could see that her real assets were in human lives, not dollars. "To ask you for money for myself is a very hard task to do...[but] I am needing funds badly."[29]

CHANGING TIMES

The TCHAS, too, was in dire financial straits and still struggling with the Great Depression; diapers, linens, clothes and even food were all in short supply. By now the oldest organization of its type in Texas, its Baby Home was often full, with the overflow privately boarded. Edna was gravely concerned about the fate of the many handicapped children she had to turn away for lack of room and funds. No hospital would take "defective babies"; they had to be sent back to family or to state institutions. In October 1935 alone, Edna was forced to return ten to their parents. "Just think what happened to these children after [that]," she wrote to Amon G. Carter, "either left on some one's doorstep or adopted by some innocent family that is entitled to a normal baby. Surely only misery and disappointment will follow such placements."[30]

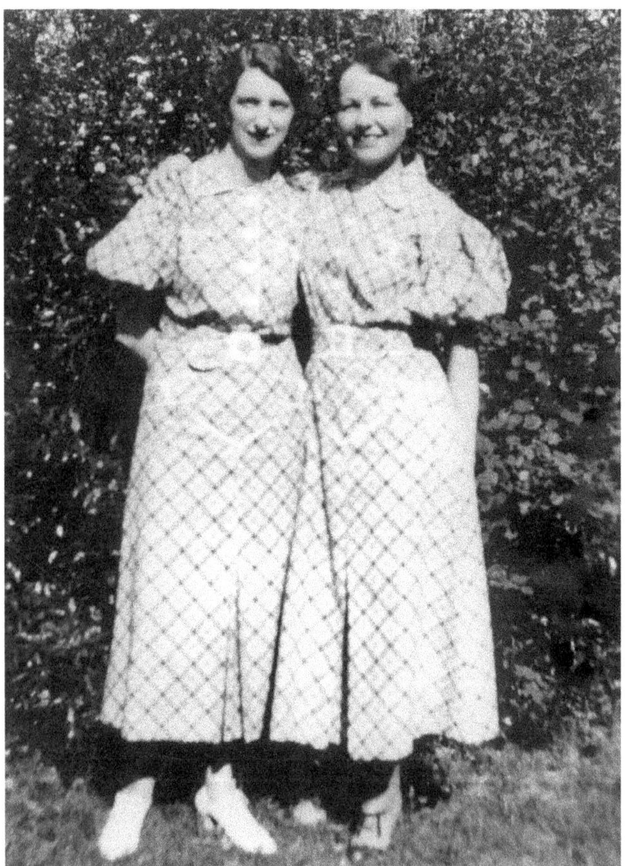

Nurses Jessie Badger and Madge Rasmussen at the Baby Home. *The Gladney Center for Adoption.*

Even placing "normal" children was a challenge. The TCHAS had more than two thousand couples on the waiting list to adopt, but preparing the children for new homes was costly, quite different from the days when Reverend Morris entered names and the few known facts about each child into a grocery ledger. "We have learned much in the past ten years," she would write to Ralph Wheelwright in 1940. "It is necessary now to verify the names, secure birth certificates, school reports, marriage certificates, death certificates, psychological tests, everything and anything that will help assist the [adoptive] parents in the proper care...of the child."

And by now, most of those two thousand waiting couples wanted a baby or toddler rather than an older child. Why the sudden interest in younger adoption? Prosperity was slowly returning to parts of America and, Edna believed, people were "tired of jazz life, [they] long for a home, a fireside and babies."[31]

In 1937 and 1939, the Texas legislature again tweaked the law eliminating "illegitimate" from birth certificates. Now, on finalization of an adoption, the Registrar of Vital Statistics would make a second certificate with the child's adopted name and the names of its adopted parents—described only as parents—and seal the original; opening it required a court order. As the bill's authors wrote, "The fact that under the present law...a reflection is cast upon a child which would follow such child through life and that *such child's birth is legal and only the acts of its parents in some instances being illegal and, in such cases, the child having no control over the same,* creates an emergency [author's italics]."[32]

The legislature had—at last—heard and understood Edna's feelings on "illegitimate" children. As she noted in 1939, "This time we finally secured a birth certificate as it should be."

Thanks to her efforts and those of state social workers and interested individuals, Texas became one of only ten states to truly protect these children from curious or unscrupulous people, while keeping their records available for the parties involved.

A Modern Home

Since its inception, the major function of the TCHAS was to "place out"—adopt—children up to the age of fourteen into new homes.[33] Edna herself had found families for more than two thousand by 1940; the estimate of total numbers placed over the years was more than seven

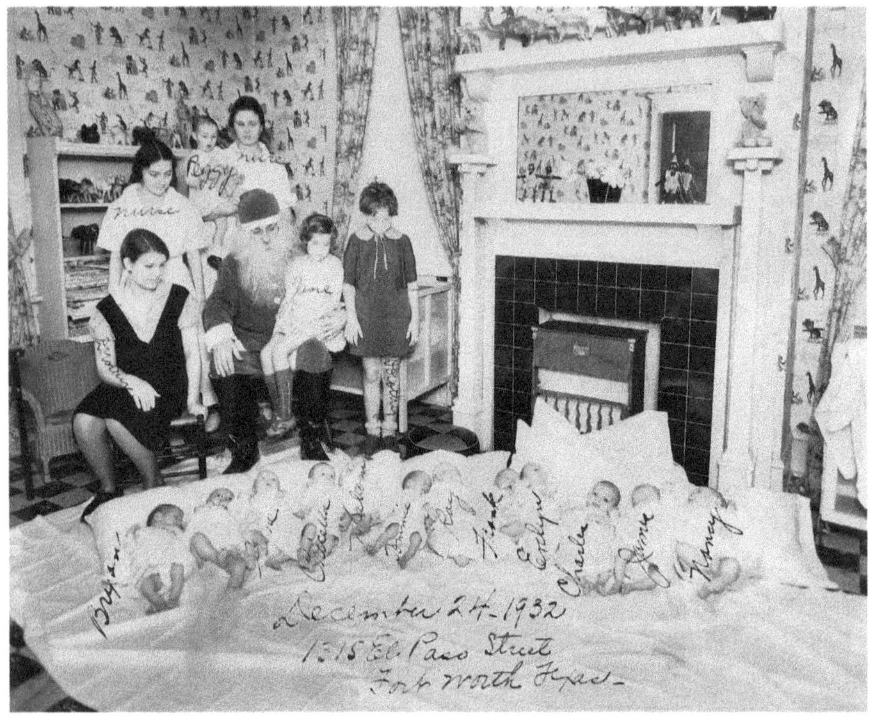

At Christmas, the Baby Home's Santa Claus often presented the infants to their new adoptive parents. *Deb Chester Maclin.*

thousand. But the times, and the needs of dependent and neglected children, were no longer what they had been in Reverend I.Z.T. Morris's day or even when Edna became superintendent. Prevailing social work theory was to keep children with their birth families as long as possible by providing skilled child welfare services to the families. The costs of this were significant for organizations such as TCHAS, especially with the large numbers of Depression-era children crowding into them.

And even in the modern 1930s, Texas's illegitimate children still faced major challenges. They were dying by the hundreds: little more than 30 percent survived their first year of life. Despite improved birth registrations, no one knew how many illegitimate babies were born in the state each year. Inadequate medical care—many such births were attended only by poorly trained midwives—and working mothers who could not be at home to breastfeed or give their children proper care were blamed. Moreover, the rate of childbirth death for unwed mothers was twice as high as for married women.[34]

Edna determined to have a very modern and healthy Baby Home. Both children and infants enjoyed plenty of health-giving sunshine and playtime in the large yards. Nurseries and bedrooms were gaily decorated in bright colors and wallpapers and furnished with books for both nurses and inquisitive young minds. The laundry staff rinsed all items multiple times, and dirty clothes were taken from a chute on the outside of the house to keep down odors inside. Harsh chemical cleaners were banned.

Edna was a follower of nutritionist and natural foods advocate Gayelord Hauser, so the kitchen had a modern electric juicing machine. Like him, she believed that fresh fruit and vegetable juice would counteract most skin problems; even the tiniest babies were fed carrot juice to thwart eczema.[35]

There were trained nurses on the staff, and local doctors donated their services to provide entrance examinations and on-going care for the children. Dr. Max Breslar, in *Blossoms in the Dust*, is a composite of several doctors associated with the Texas Children's Home, including its longtime medical director Dr. Leonidas A. Suggs and then-director Dr. Edwin G.

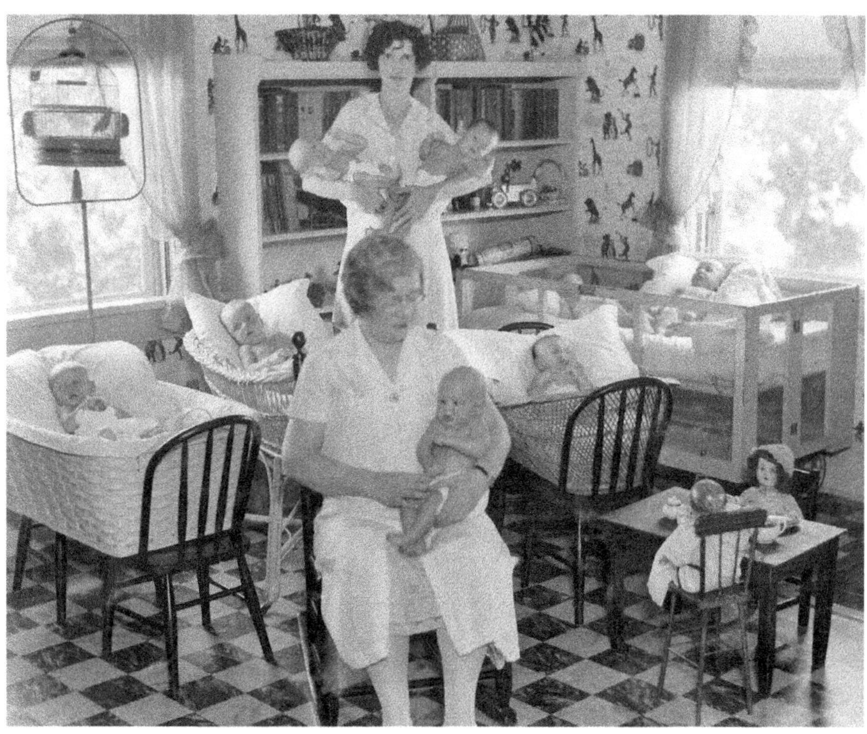

Nurses Badger and Massie with some of their charges circa 1927. The Baby Home couldn't afford many beds and used baskets instead. *Deb Chester Maclin.*

Schwarz, who specialized in diseases of infancy and childhood. Schwarz served as technical adviser to *Blossoms*, and Edna later told one reporter that "every word uttered by the doctor in the picture had been uttered by Dr. Schwarz."[36] The Home's business office was even located in Fort Worth's Medical Arts Building, where Edna had easy access to experts.[37]

Social work professionals, especially agency executives, were expected to stay *au courant* with modern methods and casework techniques. Edna's personal library contained everything from Shakespeare and works on California whales to the proper feeding of infants and children, problems of child welfare and birth control. She studied sociology at Texas Christian University as she could, but with only a small staff to fall back on, she never had time to complete the degree requirements.

ANOTHER LOSS

On June 1, 1938, Minnie Jones Kahly died of a heart attack at age sixty-eight. The loss devastated Edna. She liked to write sayings she found particularly insightful into her address books; this one best sums up her unusually strong relationship with her mother:

> *Whatever of good that is in me / Whatever of happiness I have given to others / Whatever of things good or noble I have hopes to be / In short—all that I am or will ever be / I owe to you / My mother.*

With her mother gone, Edna moved from the Worth Hotel, where she had lived since Sam's death, into Minnie's apartment at the Baby Home, bringing with her all her remaining furniture, china, silver, books and art—even a grand piano. Now it truly resembled the haven she had tried to create there: warm, comforting and far from institutional. As *Fort Worth Press* columnist Edith Alderman Guedry wrote, "She puts her whole soul as well as her pretty things into the home."

As Edna transformed her life yet again, she was no doubt horrified at the war already raging across the Atlantic.

Two days after Britain, France, Australia and New Zealand declared war on Germany, Italy and Japan on September 3, 1939, the United States proclaimed its neutrality. Congress had recently refused to pass the Wagner-Rogers Bill, which would have admitted twenty thousand Jewish refugee

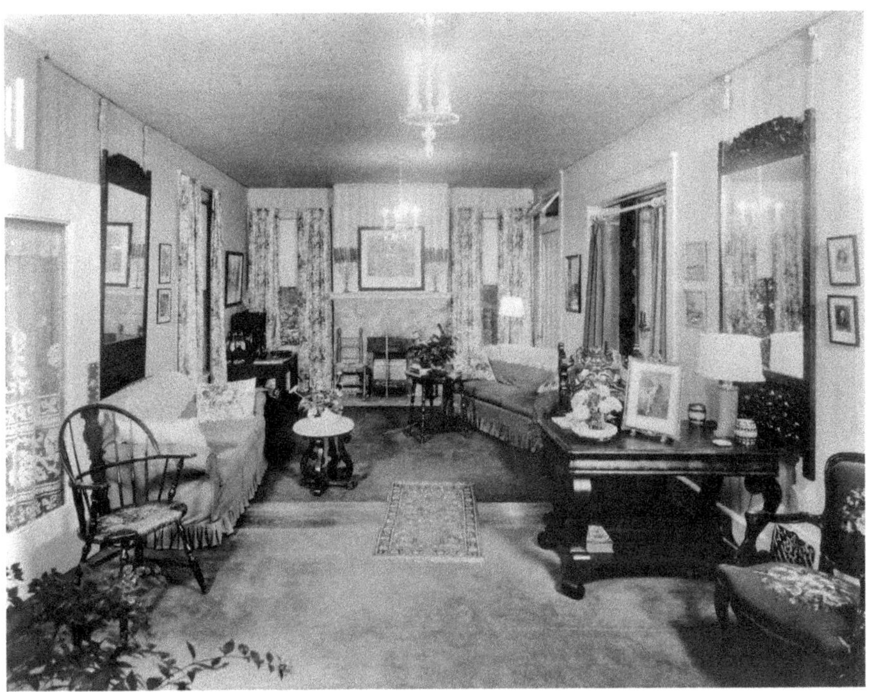

Edna furnished the Baby Home with her own furniture and belongings to make it less institutional. *Deb Chester Maclin/Warner Bros. Entertainment.*

children, an action that Edna found outrageous, particularly in light of Britain's successful "Kindertransport" rescue mission.[38]

So she was very willing to listen when Hollywood came calling and offered her a worldwide platform to talk about helpless children.

In Search of a Child

Ralph Wheelwright was a tall, handsome New Yorker in his early forties when he and wife, Phinie Louise, came to the Texas Children's Home in search of a child. After serving in World War I aboard a sub-chaser, he worked for Hearst Newspapers in Los Angeles, covering evangelist Aimee Semple McPherson and then managing publicity for William Randolph Hearst's girlfriend, actress Marion Davies. In 1930, Metro-Goldwyn-Mayer Studios hired him as assistant director of publicity. Ralph did some screenwriting,

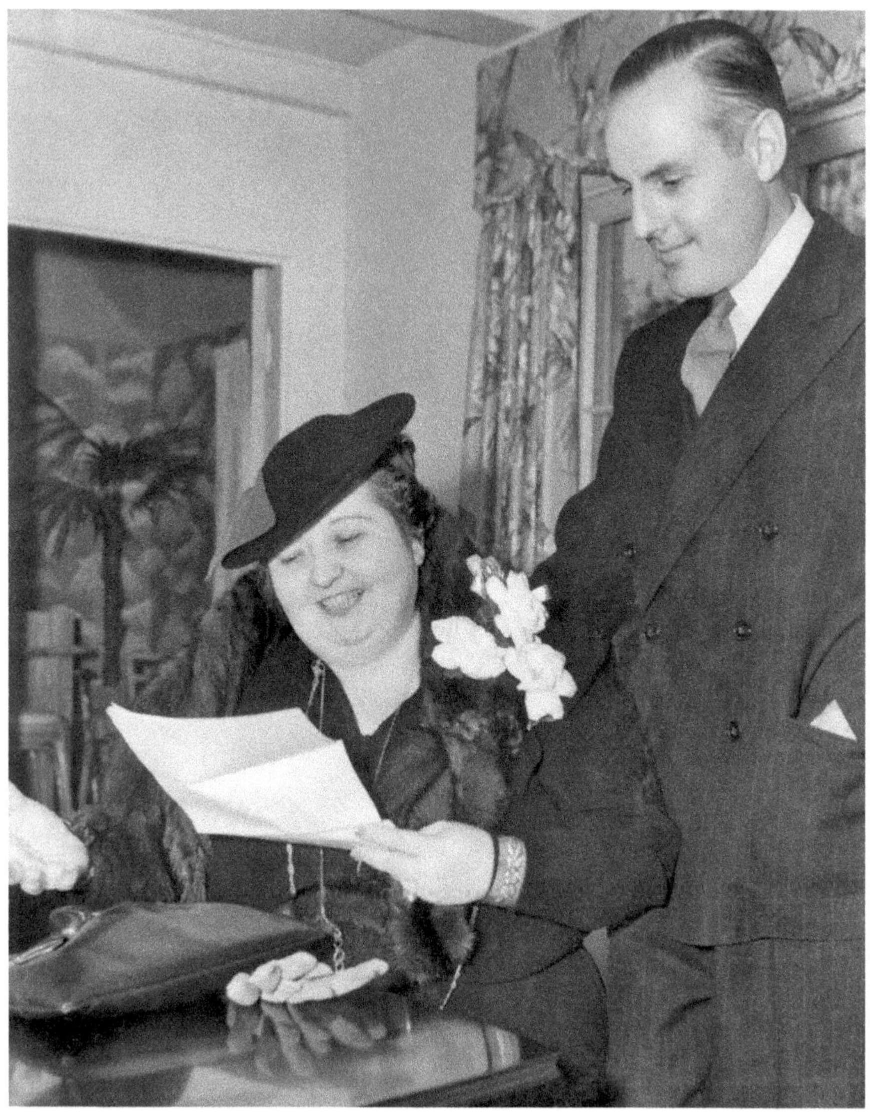

Edna and Ralph Wheelwright in MGM offices, November 1940. *Deb Chester Maclin/Warner Bros. Entertainment.*

too, including *Fast Workers* (1933), starring John Gilbert, and his first big hit, *Thunder Afloat* (1939), with Wallace Beery. He also worked in public relations and handled Clark Gable's 1937 paternity suit.[39]

Ralph and Phinie had visited the Cradle in Evanston, Illinois, but did not find the child they envisioned in their hearts. So they traveled to Fort Worth to see Edna and adopted a sprightly, precocious young girl whom they also named Phinie Louise.

With his journalistic background, Ralph probably researched the Home thoroughly before visiting it. And through his movie contacts, he likely also knew that "numerous film executives" and actors had adopted from there.[40] When he heard just a fraction of Edna's life and work and saw what she had accomplished, Ralph was hooked on her story. The canny Edna followed up by sending him newspaper clippings about the historic organization.

On April 1, 1940, he wrote her. "I was particularly interested in the clippings...and the thought occurred to me in reading them that your work may be the basis of a motion picture story. I would like to see what could be done along this line, if you would like to have me try it...It may be that the passing of the Texas law on birth certificates might be a dramatic highlight if circumstances justify."

Ralph, his wife and daughter would be traveling east in a few weeks, he continued, and he would like to "stop off and spend several days discussing story material with you." If Edna was amenable and sent him a letter of confirmation, he could register the idea with MGM before leaving. And in gratitude for her work and the Home, which had given him his treasured daughter, he would contribute 25 percent from the sale of the story, up to $5,000.

For Edna, the request could not have come at a better time: the Home was desperate for money. Fittingly, she attributed this serendipity to a child, writing to Ralph, "To think that your little girl is the means of your having helped a little organization that has struggled for over forty years...to come to our rescue just when we needed it most."[41]

Tragedies Turn into Happy Endings

What Ralph saw in Edna and the Texas Children's Home was a golden opportunity to follow MGM's highly successful 1938 film *Boys Town*, starring Spencer Tracy—who won his second Academy Award as Father Flanagan—and Mickey Rooney as the tough kid Whitey Marsh. Boys Town was a real place, founded in Nebraska in 1917, and the film was one of the first in the new genre of biography films about *living* people. The studio had actually considered a movie about the Cradle, but Ralph felt that the work of one woman was better suited to Louis B. Mayer's desire for a film also told from a woman's point of view.

With the promise of complete cooperation from Edna and the board of directors, Ralph set about putting on paper "the story of Mrs. Edna Gladney, who has mothered upon her ample bosom more than two thousand unwanted, unloved children of all faiths…and found for them homes and happiness."[42] His title, *Blossoms in the Dust*, likely came from *The Street-Children's Dance* by British poet Mathilde Blind (1841–1896). The poem speaks of the beauty of spring, then contrasts it with the lives of urban poor.[43]

> *Fathers have they without name / Mothers crushed by want and shame…Children mothered by the street…Mudlarks of our slums and alleys…Blossoms of humanity! Poor soiled blossoms in the dust!*

Armed with information from Edna, Ralph provided details about her work that today can be found nowhere else. She had adopted children into sixteen states, including Texas, and made international placements in South America, Mexico and the Philippines. Visitors to the Baby Home were often plunked down into rocking chairs and handed a baby to rock. Newborn babies were given "cradle names," which they bore until legally adopted. "Always, there would be a Franklin D. [Roosevelt], Mae [West] would be a familiar name for a buxom little lady. If a child's background was appropriate, he automatically became Dr. Schwartz, after TCHAS' benevolent pediatrician. Bald babies suggested Judge Moore, one of the adoption court jurists."[44]

In Edna's office, the hundreds of files that filled dozens of cabinets were each "a human drama…tragedies to shame man's conscience…happy endings to inspire and preserve faith in humanity."[45] One story told of a widowed musician of "mixed race" whose social and professional position recommended consideration even though he would be a single parent; for him, Edna found a sensitive and brilliant youth of the same heritage. She advised the two to correspond for several months and, in the meantime, placed the boy with a friend who had a similar home environment so that he became accustomed to it. So happy and sympathetic was the relationship between the new father and son that the boy also became an acclaimed concert pianist.

Another history was that of "a worn, gaunt woman…with a family of eight to be adopted…seven frightened youngsters from two to 13 years old. The eighth as yet unborn." Edna could place the toddlers immediately, "but the older children are not ready to be given into the kind of homes Mrs. Gladney chooses for her children. They have to learn to wear shoes. They must become accustomed to eating regularly, to better their vocabulary, put out of their little minds the stark terror of a sad beginning. The unborn baby presents no problem. Mrs. Gladney has 4,700 approved homes in the list of applications on her desk." She may even give the new baby to one particular applicant, a young woman adopted from TCHAS herself.[46]

In developing his story, did Ralph learn of Edna's illegitimacy? Probably. It would have been crucial for him to know in developing reasons for her actions, particularly in the birth certificate campaign, though he had to obscure her actual motivation. In a letter to her, he wrote, "I do not think my outline departs very much from fact but, of course, a certain amount of fiction or dramatization is necessary. However, I believe all of the fictionized incidents will have a factual basis."

From Idea to Script

Edna signed a contract with MGM that gave the studio permission to make a motion picture "dealing with your life and your experiences and with the work, lives and activities of the residents" and staff of the TCHAS, as well as to use her name and the Home's in advertising. Though the agreement also conveyed the right to change her name, Ralph and MGM chose to use her real name to give the film more veracity. In early May 1940, as the Nazis invaded France and Belgium and nylon stockings went on sale in the United States for the first time, *Blossoms in the Dust* started into production.

Ralph Wheelwright would not write the script, though his input was valued; that job went to several consecutive screenwriters. Edna was unhappy with the first script, which she felt belittled Sam's family; she also wanted to make sure that names of actual parents and of the Baby Home's donor, A.J. Duncan, would be removed. "I have a perfect horror of it being 'sickening sweet,'" she wrote in July. "You have made me much too good."

Louis B. Mayer suggested giving Edna's character more humor, building up the romance between her and Sam and stressing how the birth certificate legislation brought happiness to so many, not just in Texas, but also in other states where similar laws had since been enacted. The ending of the film then being planned was to bring the story up to date by focusing on a child's face against a backdrop of war headlines. "Everyone who has read the script so far has wept unashamedly," Ralph wrote Edna in September. "It is by far the most beautiful script ever turned out on this lot."

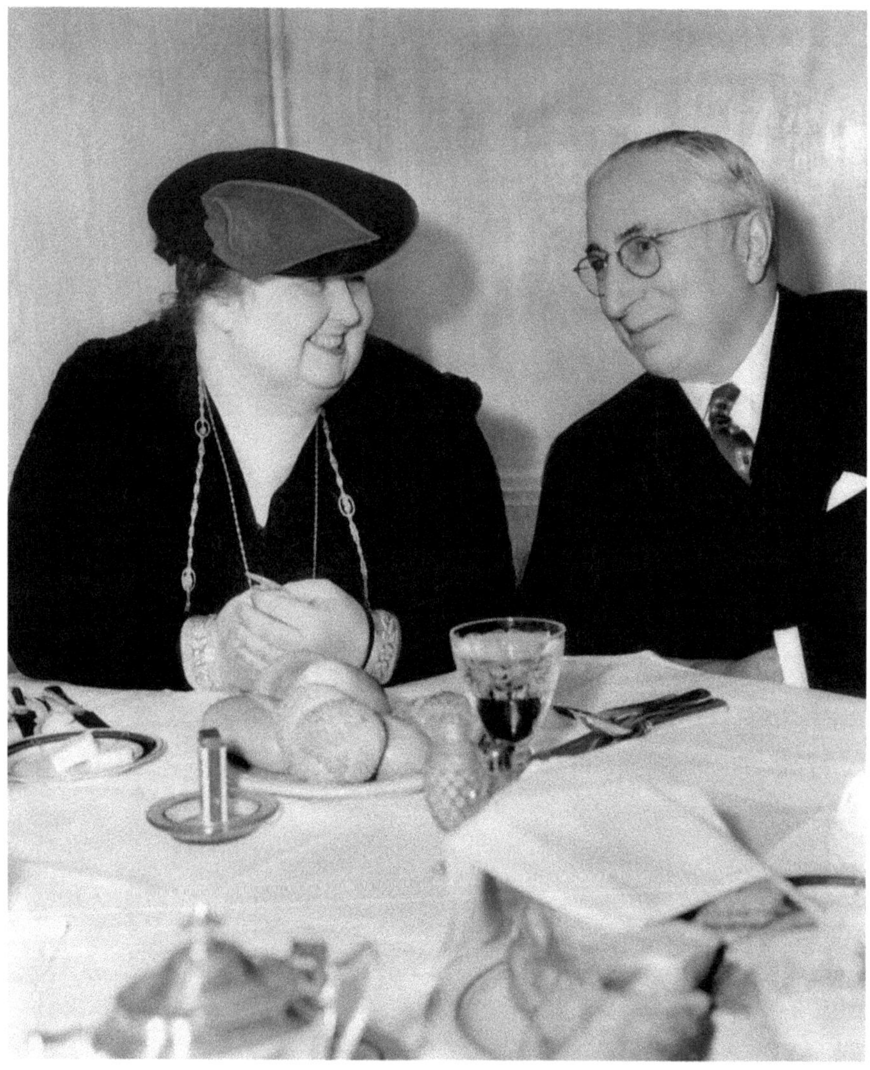

Edna enjoys lunch with MGM studio head Louis B. Mayer. *Deb Chester Maclin/Warner Bros. Entertainment.*

By now, a third screenwriter with serious credentials had been brought in to do new scenes and dialogue. The petite Anita Loos, author of *Gentlemen Prefer Blondes*, was unhappy about the assignment because "there wasn't any plot." She finally chose to focus on "a precept of Edna's that 'even the most perfect orphanage creates traumas that can hurt children for life; they should be gotten into real homes just as soon as possible.'"[47] In her memoir,

Kiss Hollywood Goodbye, Loos referred to Edna's illegitimate children quote and quipped that "MGM paid her a large sum for that single line as basis for" the film. She created the role of the handicapped boy Tony as a symbol of all the children Edna had helped and loved.[48]

That "large sum" proved to be $5,000, nearly $84,000 today and one-third of what Ralph received for the sale of the story to MGM. Edna promptly placed it in the Home's bank account so she could pay bills.

Playing the Part

Edna was stunned when MGM announced in June that she would be portrayed by rising star Greer Garson, a flame-haired beauty of Celtic and Scandinavian heritage discovered by Louis B. Mayer on the English stage. Greer had planned to be a teacher but worked at an advertising agency instead while she tried acting. In 1937, she appeared in *Old Music* at London's

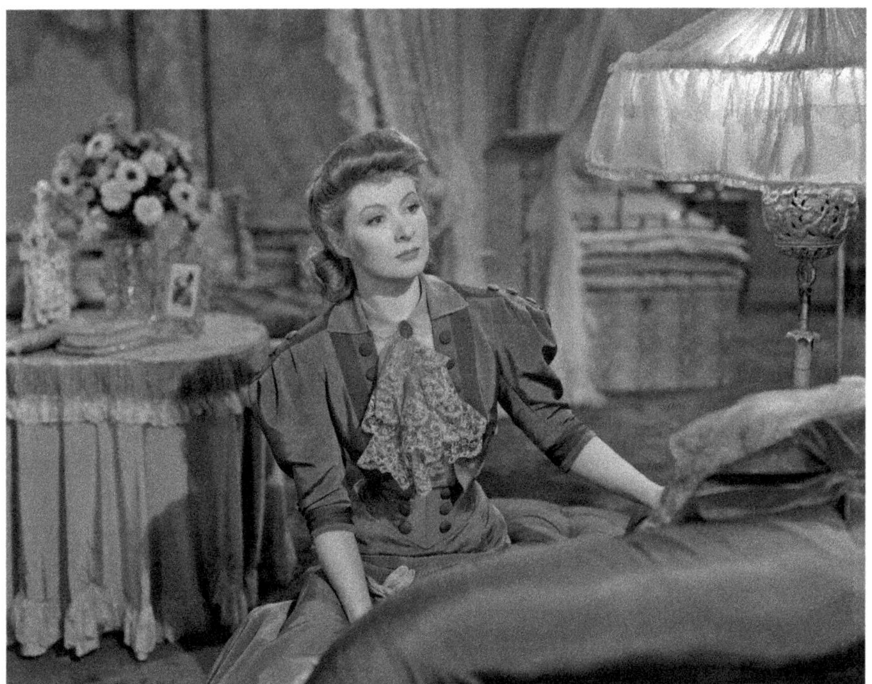

"You haven't seen anything gorgeous until your mortal eyes have beheld Miss Garson in a blue party dress," raved one critic. *Deb Chester Maclin/Warner Bros. Entertainment.*

St. James Theater, and Louis B. Mayer happened to be in the audience one night. She joked later that he had thought it was a musical; otherwise, he might not have attended. He quickly signed her to a contract and brought her to Hollywood.

But it was a year before he put her in her first movie, *Goodbye, Mr. Chips*, for which she received her first Best Actress nomination. *Pride and Prejudice* with Laurence Olivier soon followed. Mayer considered Edna Gladney to be a "prestige role" for which Garson's dignity and femininity were perfect. The MGM publicity department would also promote her physical similarity to the young Mrs. Gladney. The now very plump Edna promptly put the actress's photo on her desk and told friends that Garson was "Edna Gladney Streamlined—and I hope she will never see me."[49]

For the role of Sam, Edna put in her vote for fellow Milwaukeean Spencer Tracy, of whom she was an "extravagant admirer." MGM was considering British actor Ian Hunter, who had recently appeared in *The Adventures of Robin Hood* and *The Little Princess.* But concern that he would return to England at any moment for war work led them in the early fall of 1940 to choose handsome Canadian singer/dancer/actor Walter Pidgeon, who resembled Sam in size and build.

Injured during World War I while in a unit of Canadian Field Artillery, Pidgeon eventually went to Boston and worked in a bank to support his singing lessons at the New England Conservatory of Music. He was discovered by Fred Astaire and bounced back and forth between Broadway and Hollywood for some years. Pidgeon had played detective Nick Carter in three films and most recently appeared in the well-received *Flight Command* with Robert Taylor.

Garson and Pidgeon's on-screen charisma would prove so magical that *Blossoms in the Dust* became the first of eight films they made together. Fittingly, the last was 1954's *Scandal at Scourie* about illegitimate and orphaned children and adoption.

MGM pulled out all the stops on the supporting cast. Felix Bressart, who flashed to fame in *Ninotchka*, would play Dr. Breslar, TCHAS's physician; he had recently appeared in *Shop Around the Corner* and *Comrade X*.

Andy Hardy's "mother," Fay Holden, was selected as Edna's mother; her real-life husband, David Clyde, was the Kahlys' butler—the first time the two had appeared together in a film. Edna's father was played by Samuel Hinds, already famous as Dr. Kildare's screen father. Marsha Hunt, one of the Bennett sisters in *Pride and Prejudice*, had the small but crucial role of Charlotte, Edna's fictional foster sister.

Irving Asher, newly returned from managing Warner Brothers' English studios and now with MGM, signed on as producer. His career dated to the silent film era, and he had completed *The Four Feathers* before coming home to the United States. Asher's first job for MGM was to produce *Billy the Kid* with Robert Taylor, which premiered less than two months before *Blossoms*.

To direct, Mayer chose Mervyn LeRoy, who was well known for such films as *I Am a Fugitive from a Chain Gang*, *Little Caesar* and *Waterloo Bridge*, as well as for producing *The Wizard of Oz*. LeRoy would later say that, of his seventy-five films, *Blossoms* and *Fugitive* were two he was most proud of for their social significance and impact on the world.

Karl Freund, another silent film veteran (including the acclaimed *Metropolis*), had photographed *Camille* and *The Good Earth* and directed photography on Greer Garson's *Pride and Prejudice*; he was chosen to also do *Blossoms*. Musical scoring was by Herbert Stothart, a Milwaukee native, who started on Broadway with Hammerstein and Gershwin. He was MGM's first musical director to win an Oscar for the enchanting *Wizard of Oz*. Rounding out the main players behind the camera was legendary art director Cedric Gibbons, who, to paraphrase MGM, had dressed more sets in Hollywood than there were stars in the sky.

Edna immediately began writing letters to these strangers who would bring her story to life. She hoped Greer Garson's performance would help spread word of the needs of refugee and deserted children, a message that she had been unable to disperse herself, though "I have done the best that I could," she wrote to the actress. "Why, precious girl, you have a chance to show to the world more on this subject than anything in the history of the world."[50] Garson, beginning in turn a friendship that would last until Edna's death, declared it "a very great privilege…to be chosen to portray your image on the screen." Writing just a few days before Germany, Italy and Japan signed the Axis Pact, the actress hailed Edna's story as "an example of loving kindness and pure unselfish service at a time when the rising tide of brutality and evil forces threatens to swamp our lives and thoughts." She also mentioned the current issue of *Life* magazine with its cover photo of a baby injured in the London bombing. "In a world that is so unbelievably cruel to little children, it would be a welcome relief to tell people [your] story."[51]

Edna's embarrassment at her present weight led her to caution Ian Hunter, who had only seen the young Edna Kahly in photos. "I certainly wanted to prepare you about my unattractive size and save you from a heart attack…consider my size as I do the Salvation Army's dress—as an emblem of service—rather than style."[52]

To Irving Asher, who was coming to visit her in Fort Worth later in the summer, she wrote that when he saw the Home and the children, "you will love your contact with them as much as I do. You can't help it."

Soon after, Edna left for several weeks' vacation in Mexico City. But even there she was on the job, locating several families interested in adopting the two Mexican babies she had in Fort Worth and keeping up with the many placements made, including that of a six-month-old "Negro" infant.

It was well she enjoyed the vacation because Edna Gladney was about to "Go Hollywood" in a really big way.

Chapter 5

Technicolor Meets Greer Garson

Studio and filming commitments kept Greer Garson, Irving Asher and others from visiting Edna in Fort Worth as they had first planned. Instead, MGM arranged for her to travel by train to Tinsel Town in November 1940 and consult on the movie. In the days before the trip, Edna was so thrilled and enthused that she declared that she was of little use to anyone at the office, and Ralph Wheelwright, who knew about the near-fifty-five-year-old's health problems, cautioned her not to wear herself out. "Try not to get excited about anything and do not feel called upon to rush around while you are here. There will be plenty of time for everything."[53]

Luckily, he didn't know about Garson's and Pidgeon's plans for Edna. Hollywood columnist Louella Parsons reported that the two "personally are going to see her visit isn't all business" and that she would see all the sights. "So everyone is looking forward to meeting this charming woman who has done so much for orphans."[54]

"The Heroine of Texas"

Accompanied by *Fort Worth Star-Telegram* columnist Ida Belle Hicks, who would document the trip for the newspaper, Edna arrived in Los Angeles to be met by a throng of TCHAS adoptive parents and their children—the Wheelwrights among them. First on the agenda was lunch with MGM's

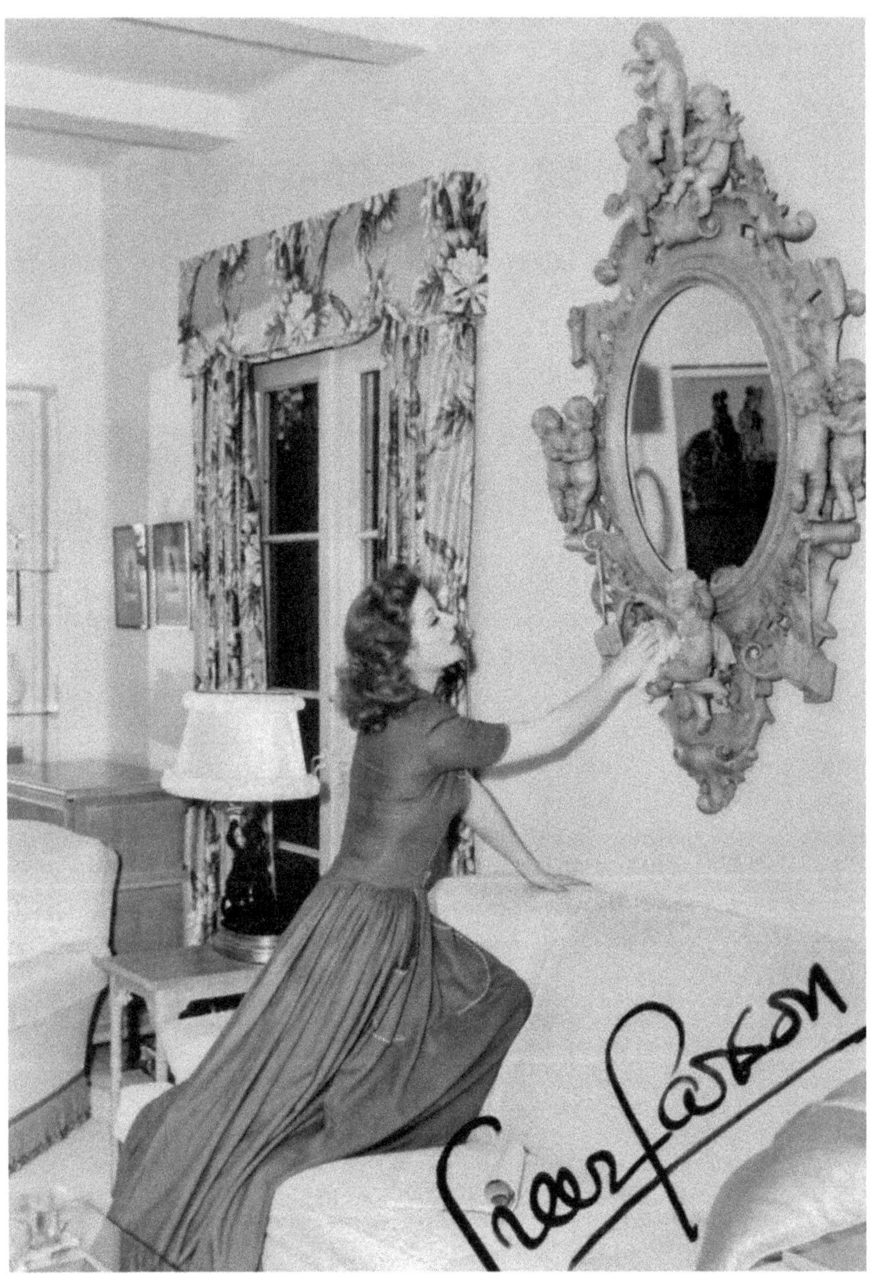

Greer Garson hung this mirror embellished with cherubs in her Hollywood home as a nod to *Blossoms'* theme. *Deb Chester Maclin/Warner Bros. Entertainment.*

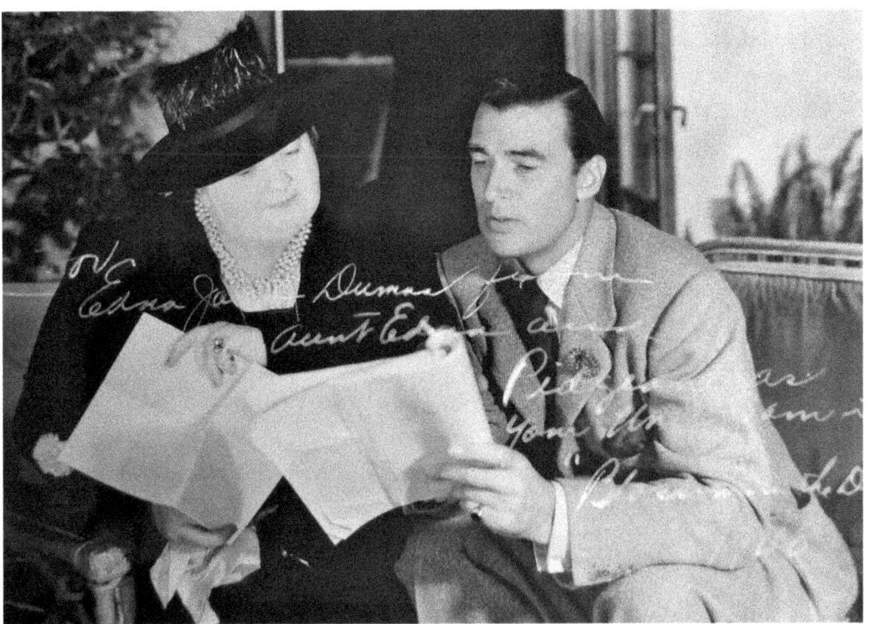

Handsome Walter Pidgeon autographed this photo for Edna's niece, Jane Dumas, then fourteen. *Deb Chester Maclin/Warner Bros. Entertainment.*

legendary boss, Louis B. Mayer, who had taken a personal interest in Edna's story and considered *Blossoms* "one of the most important productions on the forthcoming schedule."

Then it was off to Greer Garson's house for tea. She and her mother, who had accompanied her to America, had recently tired of their "quite hideous" rented furniture and redecorated primarily in white, including a large mirror surrounded by cherubs, which she had purchased in honor of Edna and *Blossoms*.

Walter Pidgeon invited the visiting Texan to tea as well when he returned a few days later from an Arizona vacation. A proper English butler and a proper English tea awaited her, but when Pidgeon asked Edna what she'd like in her tea, she smiled sweetly and said "three fingers." The actor roared with laughter and had the butler take away tea and bring in a cocktail tray.[55]

MGM spared no expense in entertaining "the heroine of Texas." Edna enjoyed a plush, flower-bedecked suite at the Ambassador Hotel, which had opened in 1921 on twenty-four acres along Wilshire Boulevard and was famous for its Coconut Grove nightclub.[56] *Blossoms* producer Irving Asher and his wife, silent film star Laura LaPlante, hosted a dinner for Edna one night at the Grove. Ida Belle Hicks reported back to Fort Worthers that their hometown heroine was treated like "a visiting prima donna."

Greer Garson later recalled that Edna charmed the cast and MGM officials, who found her "a delight—a sweet, peachy lady."[57] Anita Loos apologized for not visiting and explained, "I could not elbow my way through all the boys you attracted. Really, nobody ever made a greater sensation in Hollywood, and you have been a large part of studio conversation ever since your visit. I am trying hard to get something of your wit and exuberance into my screen play."[58] A few weeks later, Loos wrote in Hedda Hopper's column that "it was a fascinating experience to watch the two women [Greer and Edna] talk together…Here was a woman who had lived her life, chatting with a woman who would live that life on the screen."

A few weeks after her visit, director Mervyn LeRoy also wrote, saying that his thoughts had been with her and Sam since she left. "Cannot tell you what a thrill it was to meet you out here and to realize the great things that a woman like yourself is doing in this world, if we can really call it a world, today." The script, he continued, would be finished in time for Christmas, and then, "I start filming your life."[59]

A DRASTIC CHANGE IN PLANS

In October, photographer Karl Freund had made color photos of Greer Garson for a short movie promotional reel. Amazingly, it was the first time she had been photographed in color, and the results were so eye-popping that Freund immediately showed them to Mervyn LeRoy. The director "was stunned by the Garson coiffure, which glowed like a misty dawn," and contacted Irving Asher. The two decided that a Greer Garson film in black and white was practically a waste of the actress's red hair, green eyes and porcelain complexion. The *Oakland Tribune* mused that this was "probably Hollywood's first try at redesigning an entire film to match a star's hair."[60]

Immediately, set construction was halted and plans were made to film *Blossoms* with relatively new three-reel Technicolor film. This color process was first developed in 1917 and modified several times over the years; because of the high cost, it was for decades only used as inserts into black and white films. Technicolor required a tremendous number of lights and large, cumbersome cameras; the color range was also limited, but the three-reel system now offered sharp reds and blues. Part of the expense of the process lay in having to rent all the cameras and an on-site color expert from the Technicolor Company.

Few actions are as demonstrative of MGM's commitment to *Blossoms in the Dust* as the decision to change to Technicolor, since it cost both time and money. (And this at a time, too, when the war in Europe had all Hollywood in "violent jitters," not knowing what would happen to their industry or their international markets.) Sets had to be completely redecorated for color film, and both Karl Freund and art director Cedric Gibbons were determined not to use the bright, almost garish hues that were fine for musicals and outdoor locations but not for a dramatic movie about babies. "Since we are shooting in color solely to make the most of Miss Garson's looks," Freund told the *Danville (VA) Bee*, "the sets must flatter her coloring."[61] At the same time, the backgrounds had to be neutral and pastel enough to allow the actors to stand out.

Set and costume designers pored over color charts for two months and even invented colors that weren't in them; in all, 291 colors and tones were used. The final scheme was based on shades of grey with reds, blues and greens added. Technicolor made the food in dining scenes look unappetizing, so items were diluted with other foods to appear edible. Costumes—particularly Greer Garson's—had to enhance the actors' skin tones. (Then Karl Freund discovered that her deep blue outfits, when combined with the bright Technicolor lights, turned her eyes from green to blue.) Even the Gladneys' dog became a dark red Irish setter named Copper to better blend with the furniture. But the effort was worth it. "For the first time, homes and offices and streets appear entirely normal and not something off an artist's palette…realism in color was the goal."[62]

Technicolor cameras weren't the only new gadgets to be used; Walter Pidgeon proved to be allergic to the huge carbon lamps that lit the sets. And MGM's sound director was testing a new six-way microphone for the first time. It could be adjusted minutely to eliminate or soften background noises, especially babies crying.

The children playing in the backgrounds of scenes were perplexed by another bit of "technology." Their enticing horns, rattles and bells made absolutely no sound: the prop department had carefully removed the fun, noise-making parts so dialogue in the foreground could be heard.

During this interim, screenwriters continued to fine-tune the script (yet another writer reworked early scenes while Loos completed the rest), and laborers did the same on sets. MGM had hired photographers to shoot relevant scenes, particularly buildings, in Sherman, Fort Worth and Austin.[63]

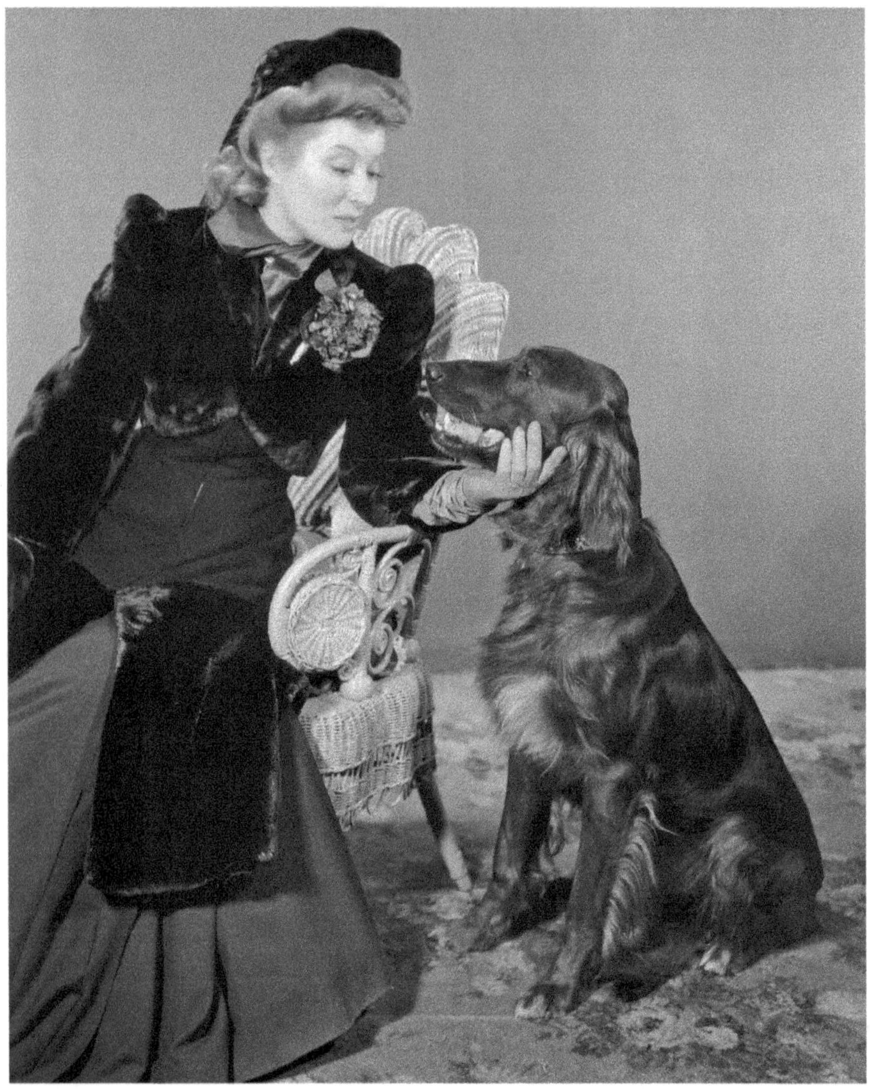

Greer Garson as Edna with Copper, the Irish setter chosen to complement her hair color. *Deb Chester Maclin/Warner Bros. Entertainment.*

The results were so precise that *Blossoms* actors later visiting the Baby Home knew exactly where everything was. The set interiors were detailed down to the wallpaper in various rooms and the spindles on the main staircase. In other scenes, such as the Fort Worth flour mill where Sam worked, glass shots or matte paintings—the so-called trick process—were used.

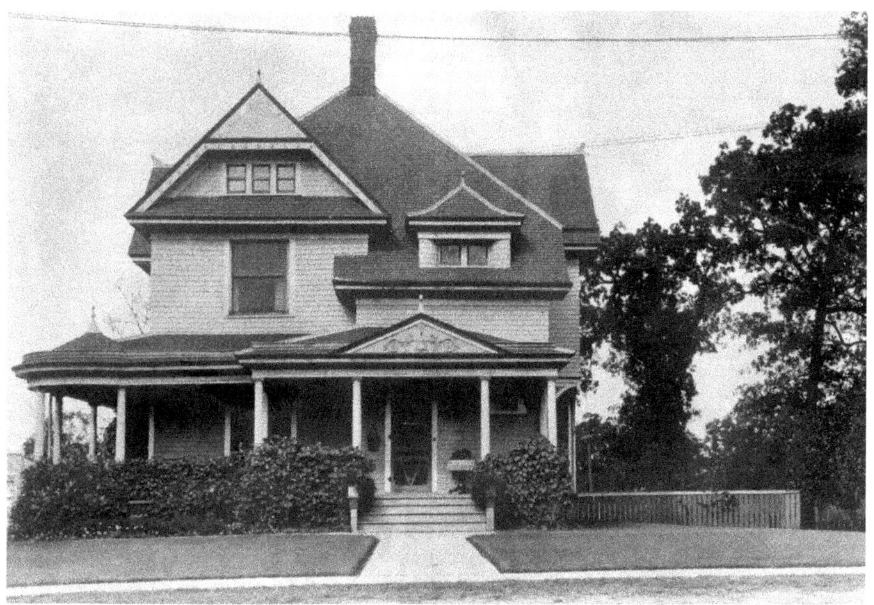

The Gladneys' first home in Sherman, on Crockett Street, still survives and was probably the basis for the house portrayed in *Blossoms in the Dust*. *Deb Chester Maclin.*

The publicity department was also hard at work building up excitement with stories of the stars and Edna's life and work. The earliest release came in June 1940 with news that Greer Garson would probably star. "So many of our movie stars have adopted children in the last few years," added the *San Diego Union*, "that it's surprising someone hadn't thought sooner of making a film about the many foundlings who are placed with [adoptive] parents annually."

Back in Fort Worth

Back in Fort Worth, Edna's work never let up despite the thrill of events in Hollywood. She often worked seventy hours a week or more and rarely took vacations, though she did enjoy traveling around the country to visit placements and check out prospective parents. Her weight and periodic bouts of poor health made this difficult. She had suffered respiratory problems since childhood—it was one reason Minnie Kahly sent her to the warmer and drier climate of Fort Worth—but she still periodically contracted pneumonia. She also had unspecified gynecological problems as a young woman, possibly as a result of the ectopic pregnancy in Cuba. And in only a few years, Edna would be diagnosed with diabetes. But even when sidelined by illness, she ran the TCHAS from her bed.

Family members who knew her from this time say that she slept poorly because of excruciating pains and cramps in her legs and often walked the floor at night. For that reason she took short "power naps" during the day, waking ready to go and moving quickly despite her size. Her cousin Mary Owen Routh laughed, saying that was the reason Edna loved going to the movies so much; in the dark, and away from ringing telephones and demands, she'd rest her head on her cane and doze off.

Raising money was a constant need. "We have never been out of debt," Edna wrote in her Christmas 1940 appeal letter, "we have taken more children than we ought; and have always been understaffed." Her fundraising weapon of choice was usually the telephone, since she disliked appearing and speaking in public. Friends and colleagues called her "a born pan-handler."[64] Routh remembered that she was strong-willed and knew how to handle people, flattering them and "making it easy for you to do what she wanted you to." More than one person received a call from Edna and promised her the needed donation, only to be asked if he could get the check to the office as quickly as possibly because they were already using whatever the item was. She was a good listener and adept at reading people but very focused on the goal she was pursuing—a true executive in a day when few women were, even in social work.

Although the Home received $7,000 a year from Fort Worth's Community Chest (about $117,000 today), Edna was constantly frustrated with its interference with her work and complaints that she couldn't stay within her budget.

Occasionally, some of her board members had the same complaint.

Dr. Grace Humphrey Hood, a longtime friend of Sam and Edna's who donated her medical services to the children for years, liked to tell the tale of Edna and John P. King, owner of King Candy Company, an old Fort Worth business. King was only one of many board members who attended meetings in the Medical Arts Building office but never visited the Baby Home. At one meeting, King complained to her, "It seems that you are too extravagant. We don't understand this. Here is a boy, eleven years old, going out [to a new home]. The price of an overcoat $19.50, a suit $6.50, shoes $7.95, sox [socks] $1.20, shirt $2.40." (The total came to $37.55 or about $634 today.)

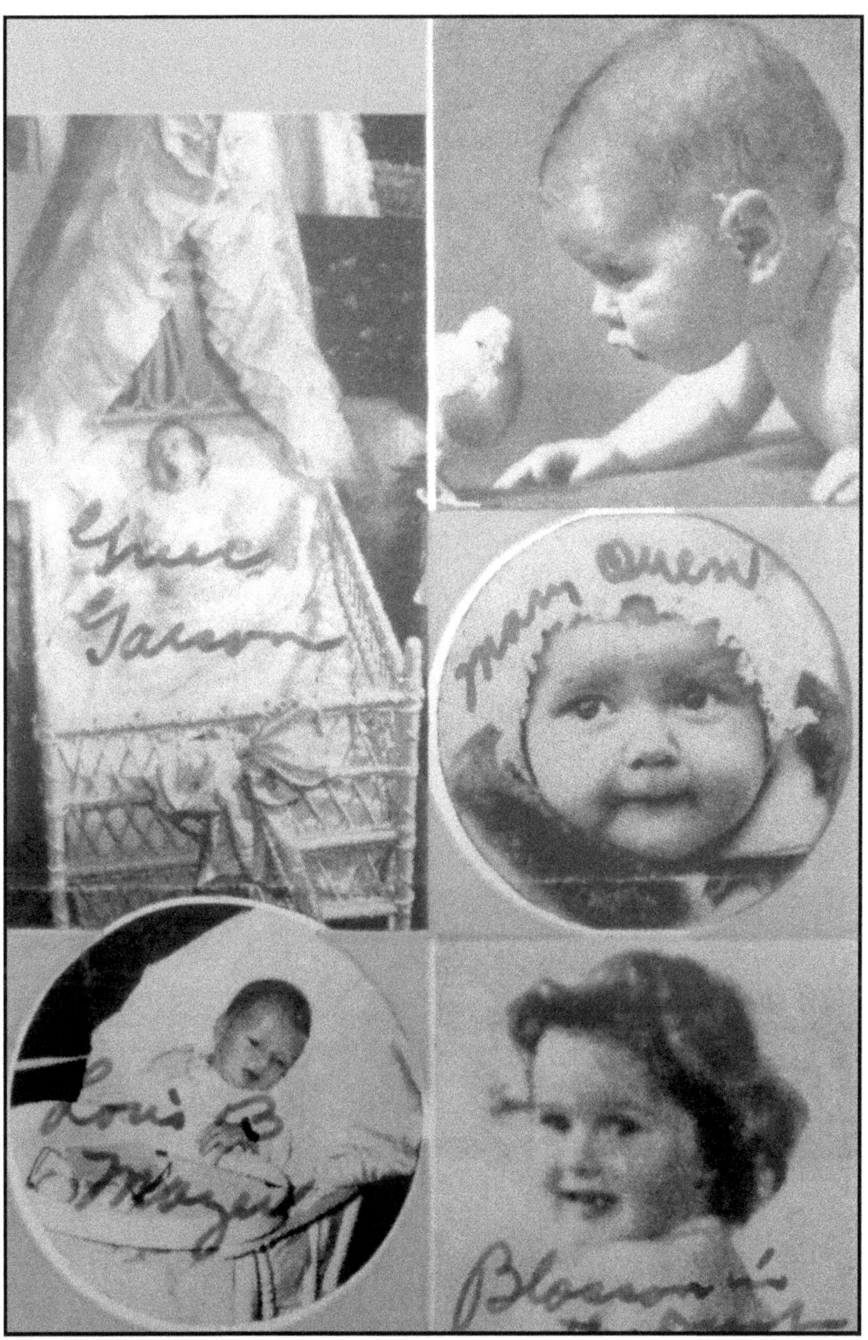

A bevy of babies with their cradle names on the cover of a Texas Children's Home brochure. *Mary Owen Routh.*

There was a long silence, and then Edna spoke:

> *Mr. King, you are president of the King Candy Company. You can tell that I like candy. I am fat. You make good candy. You wrap it, serve it in individual bonbon cups, wrap the nicer pieces in brocaded tinfoil. Your candy then is ready to be seen, except that you put it in a nice box...put a flower on the top, or a bow of ribbon, wrap it in cellophane, and put it on the market. Your candy is good. It would be just as good served in a rough, brown poke. That's the way I feel about our babies. They are just as sweet like they come to us, probably with tousled hair, dirty feet, dirty nails, unkempt in every way, but we don't like to serve our babies in a rough, brown poke. Won't you please understand that, Mr. King? I'm afraid you don't, because you have never come out to our nursery, although we have invited you a number of times.*[65]

Regrettably, Hood did not record King's reply but simply noted that "it seems some of her Board, southern men, are not as chivalrous as they are supposed to be."

MAKING A STATEMENT

Edna appreciated that one of MGM's reasons for doing *Blossoms in the Dust* was to call attention to the plight of European refugee children. But she wanted to make sure that audiences also understood that many American children suffered every day as well. "Yet in our own Texas—the largest and the richest State in the Union," she continued in her 1940 Christmas letter, "we had more than <u>seventy-five</u> thousand children poverty stricken and unable to attend school due to the lack of funds, sickness and unemployment in their families." She knew the statistics: a Child Welfare survey made in 1934 reported that at least 100,000 Texas households had no kitchen sinks, no bathtubs and no lavatories, and most still had only outside toilets.

"These children of today," she declared, "are the men and the women of tomorrow...If they are denied this chance...how can they preserve the America that we have helped make?" She closed her appeal by thanking her readers for their support of "our own Texas Refugees." She stated it a bit differently to a newspaper reporter, noting that these children would direct the state's and the country's future policies. "Unless we prepare them for this work, I am very fearful of the outcome of the future generation."[66]

Edna wanted to create an endowment fund for the Texas Children's Home so her work would continue. But it would be more than another decade before she saw that happen. She was no doubt gratified when her new friends at MGM sent in generous Christmas gifts totaling $350 (almost $6,000 today).

She sent the studio's female staff members—even L.B. Mayer's redoubtable assistant/secretary Ida "Mount Ida" Koverman—and the executives' wives sewing kits made by a Fort Worth woman. Of satin, brocade or similar fabric, the tops were gathered with a drawstring, and inside were various, small supplies; the whole fit easily in a suitcase. Some of them are still cherished by family and friends.

In January 1941, the pace of the past six months had caught up with Edna, and she retired to her bedroom to recuperate. Her secretary, Clarissa Lehman, wrote to thank Irving Asher for sending flowers: "She gets so blue some days and when she does, the entire staff just fall in line behind her and we all have the 'Texas Blues' together."[67] But by March, Edna was still sick and mentally exhausted, missing Sam in the whirl of emotions conjured by *Blossoms* and irked by difficulties with other Fort Worth social services such as Community Chest. And even before the film premiered, the Hays Office had received complaints about its subject.

The Motion Picture Production Code of 1930, commonly known as the Hays Code, was Hollywood's attempt to censure itself in the wake of many scandals. Even in the loose, postwar age of jazz and flappers, movies—in making the transition from silent to sound—had become so immoral, and the resulting outcry among the public so great, that the federal government was about to step in. Hurriedly, the industry formed the Motion Picture Producers and Distributors Association of America (MPPDA), hiring former politician and government official Will Hays as its first president. So a film about unwed mothers, illegitimate babies—85 percent of the Texas Children's Home placements were from "illicit unions"—and deserting fathers hit all the wrong buttons at the Hays Office, as the MPPDA was known, as well as at the Catholic Legion of Decency, which rated movies.

But Louis B. Mayer and Mervyn LeRoy stood firm in their belief that *Blossoms* would expose the injustice of American laws to illegitimate children. "Let the message fall where it may," LeRoy was famously quoted as saying after the film's release. "It's entertainment I'm after and if the picture has a sock or impact for humanity, so much the better."[68] Many reviewers and moviegoers agreed that *Blossoms* had presented a problem that urgently needed attention but had not done it in an unseemly manner.

Chapter 6

Oh, Babies!

Blossoms in the Dust represented a real challenge for Metro-Goldwyn-Mayer—a logistical nightmare in many ways. In addition to the 2 stars and 5 main supporting actors, 114 actors had smaller roles, most of them uncredited.

And then there were all those "blossoms in the dust"—well over eight hundred of them.

"Bugs in the Mud"

MGM began advertising in late 1940 for babies not yet born, searching for women who would be delivering in the next several months. As many as eighteen babies, only a few weeks old, were needed for some segments. Besides being in a major movie, they would earn the highest wage paid to any in the infant cast: $75 a day (about $1,200 today). In fact, the money was so significant that some of Edna's Los Angeles–area adoptive parents donated their babies' salaries to the Texas Children's Home.[69]

When the studio advertised for a four-year-old red-haired boy to play Sammy Gladney, Sam and Edna's fictional son, "the response brought 631 individual applications besides 300 more from central casting office, orphanages and dancing schools"—all in less than forty-eight hours.[70] One mother was so determined to have her son accepted that she turned up at every interview with the boy dressed in a different costume each day. Despite her efforts, the part went to a five-year-old showbiz veteran, Richard Nichols; *Blossoms* was his sixth film.

Filming the newborn Sammy required four babies working in shifts. Infants that young could work only thirty seconds at a time under the very hot Technicolor lights and no more than twenty minutes altogether in a day. And California State Labor Board regulations stipulated that all babies had to be at least two weeks old. Moreover, those under six months of age could work only two hours in the morning and two more in the afternoon. Children up to two years of age could be on the set for four hours each day but could work only two. All told, the studio employed about 100 infants and toddlers and another 650 children aged from two to eight, the largest number ever used in a single MGM film. Mervyn LeRoy joked that with so many children on the set, the crew referred to the film as "Bugs in the Mud."

The youngest babies were housed in nine sterile nurseries, one for every two babies and each with a nurse, a child welfare worker and the two infants' mothers. One MGM press release stated firmly, "There has been no baby casualty on the MGM lot for seven years, and studio heads are not going to break the record if they can help it." So much space did they require that Greer Garson and Walter Pidgeon's dressing rooms had to be moved to another set.

But babies were only part of the logistics. The 650 blossoms above the age of two were governed not only by the Labor Board's rules but also by those of the California Board of Education. For every 10 school-age children, a teacher had to be hired. Large studios such as MGM maintained a complete, year-round nursery and school on the set. There were also playrooms as well as a doctor to check the children every day. The Board of Education received a complete script with scenes marked that pertained to the children. Nurses, teachers and child welfare workers were on the set every day and had the authority to stop the filming at any time.

Little Tony

Among the children was one playing a special role. "Little Tony" figures prominently in *Blossoms*, though his character underwent many transformations as the script was developed and refined.

In Ralph Wheelwright's original story idea, red-headed Little Tony was blond, blue-eyed Little Sam, brought to the Baby Home one stormy night after his parents are killed in a car wreck. Thrown out of the car by the impact, he lies in a mud puddle for an hour before policemen find him. The result is pneumonia, which requires days of nursing by Edna and the staff. The parents are unmarried, Edna discovers, and neither family wants the baby. "Little Sam went everywhere with Mrs. Gladney…and became a part of her fight to win new adoption laws," Ralph wrote.[71] About a year later, a Michigan man comes to the TCHAS to find a child to replace his and his wife's dead son. Little Sam looks much like him.

But Edna refuses to place him; she wants to keep Sam for herself. Dr. Schwarz (Breslar in the film) reminds her that she is breaking her own rule, the one she embraced while in Sherman, to find each child the kind of home she would choose for her own child. On Christmas Eve, she learns that the birth certificate bill has passed, and she takes Sam to Michigan to his new parents. His adoption is the first to be legalized under the new law.

However, in Anita Loos's final script, and in the film, Tony first appears as a baby in a crucial scene. Edna has gone to the Tarrant County Courthouse on business for Sam and is drawn into a courtroom where adoptions are being legalized. One couple, on discovering that their intended child—Tony—is illegitimate, refuses to accept him. Edna takes him home, discovers his left leg is impaired and sets to work nursing him back to health. But none of her efforts can heal it; Tony must wear a brace for several years.

This time, when the Michigan father comes looking for a son, Edna decides to take Tony and leave, closing the Home. But a policeman appears with two children rescued in a gambling raid; one is ill, and Edna cannot bring herself to turn him away. While nursing him through the night, she realizes Dr. Schwarz was right and calls the Michigan couple to come for Tony. After he and his adoptive parents leave, she sits with the two new children as snow falls outside, and the film ends.

An unidentified newspaper columnist got a big chuckle out of that snow, particularly after MGM sent out press releases reiterating that the story had been "FICTIONALIZED CONSIDERABLY for screen purposes." That's "not only fiction but California libel," the columnist laughed.

Clearly, he had never been in Fort Worth when a "norther" blows in.

Greer Garson would later say, "Children are the most natural actors in the world. That is because they actually are not acting at all, but being themselves." But as Anita Loos recalled, Greer and "Tony" clashed one day during rehearsal. The scene has the boy about to depart with his new parents.

Tony was to acknowledge that he mustn't cry, with which "Edna" agrees. "But I can cry *inside*, can't I?" is Tony's next line. Loos recalled that even the electricians were sniffling over that, "so our star broke up the rehearsal to issue an ultimatum: unless that line was taken away from the little boy she would walk off the set." Garson argued that no child Tony's age would say such a thing, but she as an adult might tell him that he could do it. "That small actor had run up against a more powerful scene-stealer than he was," Loos wrote.

The tiff ended up in Louis B. Mayer's office. To everyone's amazement, that "tough old autocrat" cried, too, when he heard Tony say his line "and ordered it to be kept where it belonged, in the mouth of a toddler."[72]

The actor who brought Tony to life so sweetly was billed as Pat Barker. Since the character was a boy, and the name of the actor that of a boy, everyone outside the film crews thought Tony was played by a boy. It was not until after *Blossoms* debuted that MGM revealed Pat was really Patricia.

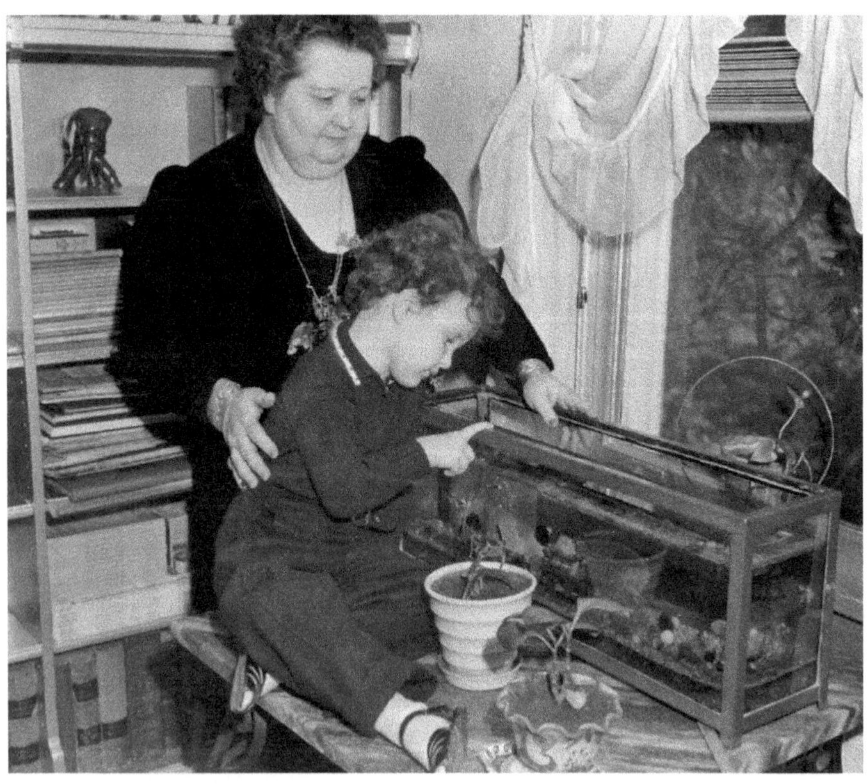

Patricia Barker, *Blossoms*' "little Tony," visited Edna at the Baby Home in the fall of 1941 and found the aquarium fascinating. *Deb Chester Maclin.*

The daughter of a ballet dancer and a Chicago insurance broker, she was naturally red-haired and had studied ballet since she could walk; by the age of two and a half, Patricia could dance on her toes. Mervyn LeRoy was delighted to find her; he'd auditioned many boys who were young enough for the part but couldn't learn all the dialogue.[73]

"A Red Letter Day"

Principal filming for *Blossoms in the Dust* began on Monday, January 27, 1941—"A RED LETTER DAY!!!" Ralph scrawled across a copy of the shooting schedule he sent Edna. First to be filmed were interior shots in the Kahlys' fictional house: kitchen, pantry, dining room and lower floor.

MGM's Press Book offered advertising ideas and sample releases to theaters, including these amusing snippet-length stories about making the film.[74]

Greer Garson set a Hollywood record for the number of different hair-dos she sported over the length of the movie: seventeen in all. That kept MGM's chief hair stylist Sydney Guilaroff very busy. Guilaroff was famous for creating the "bob" popularized by Louise Brooks, Claudette Colbert's signature bangs, Judy Garland's *Wizard of Oz* braids and ponytails and Lucille Ball's red hair. In 1938, he also became the first single man in the United States to adopt a baby. The State of California tried to stop it, but Guilaroff prevailed.

Greer wrote to Edna on February 15, 1941, that this "very serious minded, charming young man" would like an introduction to her. "He is naturally very much interested in the whole question of child adoption… he tells me that many friends of his [childless, married couples] who are anxious to adopt children encounter a great deal of obstruction on the part of child welfare authorities which makes adoption difficult, if not impossible in many cases. He is sure that with your influence you might be able to do something to relax the rigidity of the institutional mind, as he calls it, and is very anxious to write" you.

Another delightful story released by MGM was one about Fay Holden, who played Edna's mother and hated the corsets she had to wear under her Gibson Girl–style clothes. "It seemed that I spent most of my time lacing and unlacing corsets," she said. "There is only one good thing about corsets. They feel so good when you get them off!"

Mervyn LeRoy had an entire new scene written when he discovered how many famous people had been orphans. In the film, "Edna" shows guests photographs of some of them hanging in her office. They include three presidents—Rutherford B. Hayes, Andrew Jackson and Andrew Johnson—British prime minister David Lloyd George, Cardinal Patrick Joseph Hayes of New York City, evangelist Billy Sunday and educator and author Booker T. Washington. LeRoy could also have mentioned a few other famous adoptees and orphans: John James Audubon, George Washington Carver, Edgar Allan Poe and First Lady Eleanor Roosevelt.[75]

Walter Pidgeon had spent some time on the stage doing musical comedy before Hollywood beckoned. So he didn't understand why he had to have dancing lessons for an early scene at a party. "That's just the point," said LeRoy, "you have to dance badly, not well." To "help" his star, the director had a low platform built on roller skates. While other couples danced around the two stars, they bounced up and down nicely. In his autobiography, *Take One*, LeRoy recalled that Pidgeon's first words on the set every morning were "When do we eat?" He'd never seen anyone who ate so much and didn't gain weight.

SILENCE IN THE COURTROOM

One of the pivotal plot points in *Blossoms in the Dust* is the courtroom scene in which a birth father, "Bert La Verne," tries to discover the identity of his son's rich adoptive parents. He had been happy enough to dump his newborn son at the Texas Children's Home after his wife died so he could go to Mexico and run a dance hall. Edna tries to persuade him to keep little Frederick, but La Verne wants no commitment and no drama. His parting shot—"That's the trouble with you girls who never had a kid."—has doubtlessly resonated with many thousands of infertile women.

But somehow he learns that the baby has been placed in a rich family. He accuses Edna of selling little Frederick and takes her to court when she refuses to divulge the information he wants. La Verne's attorney paints him as a humble man, willing to denigrate himself to make a living and a home for his son. But even so, he tells the judge, La Verne will give up the person he loves most if he can just see his son and be sure he's all right.

Edna and Judge Hartford have been exchanging long, eloquent looks. He acknowledges that the law allows such information if the birth parent

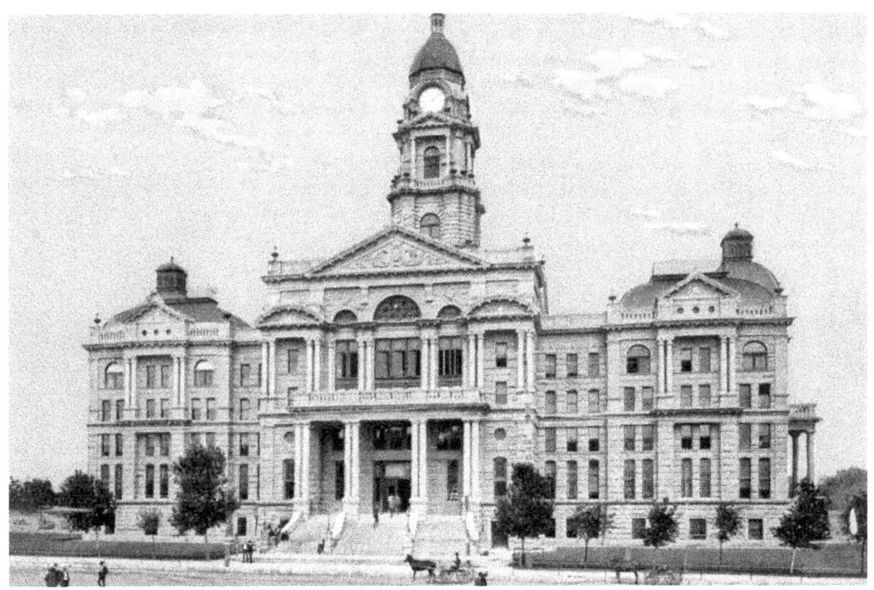

Opened in 1895, the Tarrant County Courthouse in Fort Worth is where most Gladney adoptions are still finalized. *Author's collection.*

has reasonable doubts about the family with whom the child was placed. Solemnly he tells Edna she must divulge the names. Silently and firmly, she shakes her head "no." Then, the judge states, he has no choice but to find her in contempt and send her to jail. Still she refuses. At last, Judge Hartford realizes he has an escape; he declares he is not qualified to try the case and will have it transferred to another court. As he leaves the courtroom, Dr. Breslar realizes the truth—the judge is the adoptive father.

This scene is based on an actual case brought against Edna and TCHAS by a birth mother. As reflected in Ralph Wheelwright's original story idea, "one of the State's outstanding legal minds, formerly a high public official, sprang to Mrs. Gladney's defense." But when asked to reveal names, Edna rises and declares, "In the interest of this child's happiness, I must refuse, your honor." The judge, who knows Edna well and senses a loophole he can use, delays sentencing until 2:00 p.m., when she must produce the records. Sam Gladney, whose presence in this scenario indicates the trial happened prior to his death in 1935, asks where the records are and takes her filing cabinet key. Edna's attorney protests that he cannot destroy the records or take them out of the court's jurisdiction. Sam smiles and says he's just going fishing.

The TCHAS Board of Directors meets hurriedly, fearful that her actions will "attract sensational publicity." A tired and heartsick Edna tells them they won't have to ask her to resign. "If I can't stop this outrage, I would never want to place another child in a home to face such a tragedy." She returns home to pack for a jail stay. Back in the courtroom, her attorney anxiously watches the door. "Finally, the venerable figure of the presiding judge of one of Texas' highest tribunals entered and approached the bar." He has pertinent information—he decreed the adoption fourteen years earlier—and wishes to testify. Returning the girl to its birth mother would be tragic, he declares, and the court agrees, dropping the contempt charge.

In Ralph's retelling of the story, it is Edna's defense attorney who is the adoptive father. And she takes away from the experience a very clear lesson: "We are not finished when we have found homes and names for our children…It is our duty to ensure and protect their futures."

So how much of this story actually happened? Ralph's version is probably closer to the truth than what was portrayed in *Blossoms*. From Edna's correspondence with MGM, it's clear the main protagonist was a birth mother, but the author has been unable to find the actual court records. (The birth mother also tried to extort money from either TCHAS or MGM.) However, a letter from Edna's personal attorney, Charles Kassel, to Louis B. Mayer relates that he, Kassel, took part in the trial "and for my pains in that regard found my office safe opened and rifled that night."[76] Cecil Hubbert, another local lawyer connected to the Texas Children's Home, served as Edna's attorney in the contempt proceedings.

Chapter 7

"Today You Are a Very Famous Woman"

Blossoms in the Dust ended filming in early April 1941, slightly delayed by Greer Garson's falling ill with strep throat. Even then, there remained editing, musical scoring, retakes and other tasks. "Try not to be impatient," Ralph jokingly wrote to Edna. She was still largely housebound, going to the office only occasionally on important matters and conducting remaining business from her apartment at the Baby Home.

War Babies

From the project's beginning, *Blossoms* had been intended as a way to publicize the horrors being faced by European refugees, especially children, by calling attention to the thousands of unwanted and neglected young ones around the world. Even peppery-tongued syndicated columnist Hedda Hopper had an opinion on that. "There's never been a time in the history of this world when so many children were hungry, afraid and alone as today. We can't all build homes for them, as Mrs. Gladney did, but we can make pictures about them, which I'm certain will help."[77]

Edna had already expressed her opinion in a letter to Greer Garson, shortly after it was announced that the actress would star in *Blossoms* and only days before the Battle of Britain began. "We will all be asked to take the Refugee children, and I hope that every family will…for the duration of the war. These children come to us unafraid, looking for protection and [a] love [which has] no malice or envy, greed or hurt or guns."

As President Franklin D. Roosevelt tried to put the United States on a war footing, Hollywood movie studios were stymied about how to best portray the situation. It was impossible for them to depict "American soldiers in battle because there were as yet no American soldiers at the battlefront."[78] Even as the *Blossoms* script was being written, however, Congress enacted the first American military draft in peacetime on September 16, 1940, so it was clear that the United States could indeed be in a war. Edna, who had already been through one, knew what that meant.

Fort Worth had practically been an armed city during World War I with the presence of army training facility Camp Bowie, Camp Taliaferro (a flight training center) and several airfields. The inevitable result was brothels, saloons and other "entertainment" springing up around each one, with a consequent rise in crime, illegitimate births and venereal disease. VD was also strongly prevalent in European battle zones, and the fear was that American troops would return to infect their loved ones here.

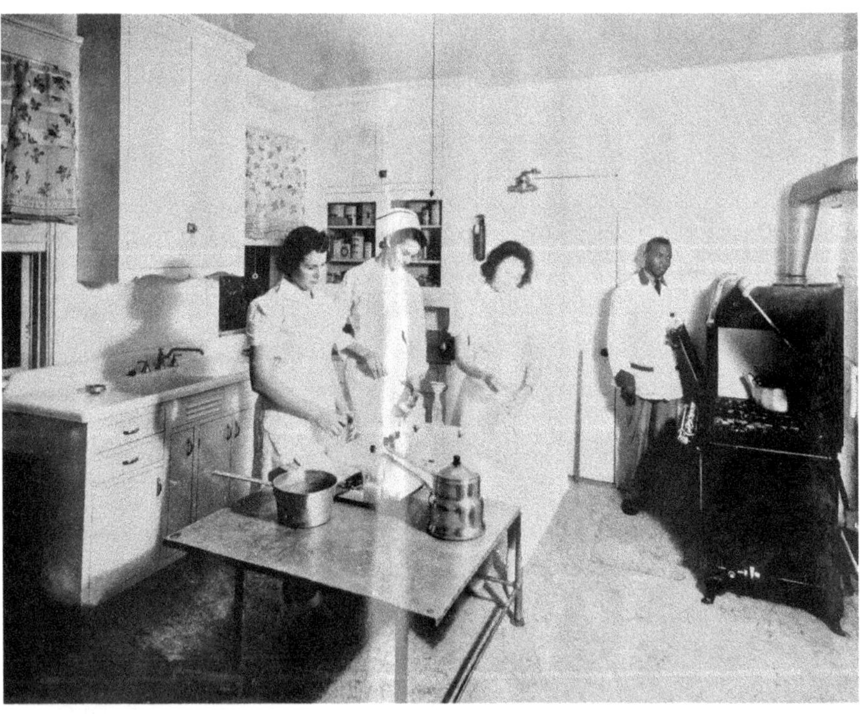

Preparing formula and meals in the Baby Home's spacious and sanitary kitchen. *University of California at Los Angeles/Special Collections.*

Edna could now see the same cycle beginning once more. The earlier camps were gone, but Fort Worth was well known as an aviation center, and there were several pilot training schools in the area. It seemed reasonable to expect that the looming war would bring more military attention to the city and, consequently, an increase in young women needing her help.

She would be widely quoted on this subject in interviews about *Blossoms in the Dust*. Americans, she declared, "do not realize that an emergency is at hand in our own country right now. That emergency centers around our own war babies, and yet we are not at war." For those who failed to understand, she explained the problem: money. "But with so many of our boys in [military] camp with only $21 [salary] a month and unable to help expectant mothers, the situation is very serious."[79] Whether these mothers were wives or unwed mattered not to Edna: the fact remained that they were in trouble. And many of them would be turning up on her doorstep for advice and help in finding homes for their children.

Edna had probably begun to think of transforming the TCHAS from only a placing-out agency to a modern adoption agency that also operated a maternity home for unwed mothers. Society had changed, and so had its rules. Young women were no longer courted in their parents' presence. The mobility and privacy granted by the automobile, the wider world that could be seen on movie screens and the rapid demographic shift from rural to urban America had changed all those rules. What hadn't changed were the consequences of an unplanned or undesired pregnancy. Social workers knew the situation would worsen dramatically if war did indeed come.

Edna wanted understanding for the terrified young women who came to her in secrecy and shame and gave birth to children who would ultimately be loved by other women. "All the brave soldiers are not wearing the Croix de Guerre," she said emphatically, "for it took real nobility of character for those mothers to answer in detail all the questions I asked."[80] Nor did she believe in Texas's long tradition of letting birth fathers off the hook; she made every effort to locate them and get a medical history and blood test for the child's sake.

The coming war—and its innocent victims—would soon overwhelm the Texas Children's Home.

"Today You Are a Very Famous Woman"

While Edna prepared for the onslaught she knew lay ahead, MGM was in the last stages of readying *Blossoms in the Dust* for release.

On May 7, Ralph wrote to Edna that the studio took the movie "out in all its rough and incomplete form to a little neighboring town and ran it as a 'sneak' preview…it is the most beautiful picture I have ever seen and…the audience reaction was wonderful…so inspiring, and in such good taste. Mrs. Wheelwright [his wife, Phinie Louise] was in tears at the finish and everybody else was dabbing [their eyes with] handkerchiefs." Ralph himself was probably in tears, too, since this was his first viewing of the project he believed in so strongly. "I know you have a wonderful picture," he continued passionately, "one that should inspire and touch the hearts of every person who sees it, to encourage the interest of people in the problems of child adoption…to make [people] happy…and proud…that there are in America women like Edna Gladney." He went on to tell her that one woman in the preview audience had said, "I feel GOOD for having seen that picture."

Everyone at MGM was delighted with the reviews. Irving Asher telegraphed Edna with the news that over four hundred audience response cards praised the beauty of *Blossoms* and its subject—an important point after the negative letters sent to the Hays Office. All that remained now was to insert music and some special effects, "after which [the] picture goes into [the] laboratory" for processing. "You are going to love it," Asher assured Edna.

MGM had arranged for her to see the film before any kind of release, and Asher personally flew to Fort Worth in his private plane to bring the print to her. She was flabbergasted to walk out of the Baby Home and find him sitting in the front yard. On Thursday, June 19, friends of the Ashers, Mr. and Mrs. Edmund Schenecker, drove her to Dallas's Renaissance Revival palace—the Majestic Theater—to see her life unfold on the big screen.

Edna sat alone in the projection booth and, so far as is known, never shared with anyone the conflicting emotions that must have overwhelmed her.

Directly afterward came the press showing of the movie, and Ralph hastened to send her news of it, too. Hard-boiled newspaper critics wept, he reported with delight. "Today you are a very famous woman. You will be more famous in the days to come." To Edna, he could express his innermost feelings about the subject and the movie he'd brought to life. "It has been a long, long road. I have had many moments of great worry. But now, after all, here is a picture far beyond my fondest hopes…I sincerely hope that my own complete satisfaction reflects the warmth that is within your own

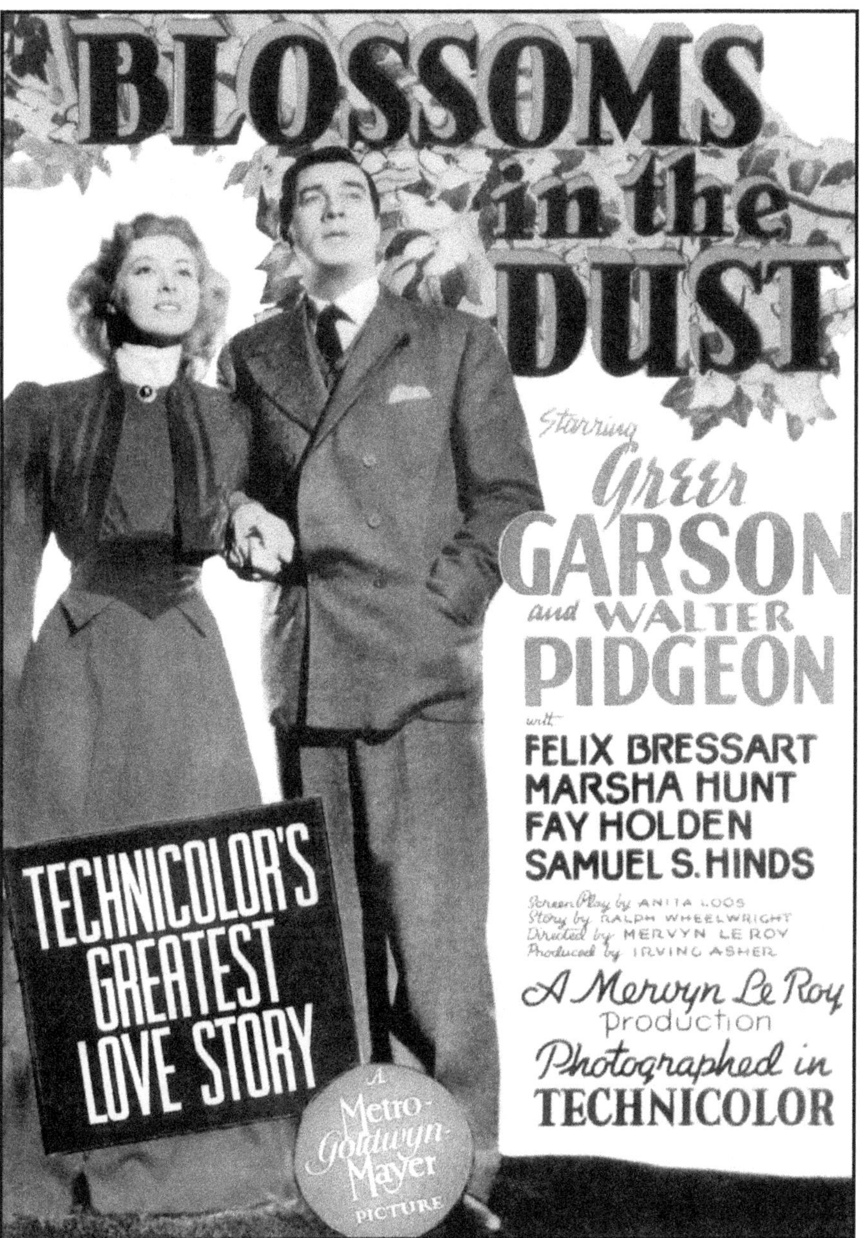

Metro-Goldwyn-Mayer suggested that theaters emphasize the romance of Sam and Edna's story in their local advertisements. *Gladney Center for Adoption/Warner Bros. Entertainment.*

heart at this proud moment." He'd been inspired, he wrote, by the daughter Edna had given him and his wife. "Whatever everybody else did was merely physical effort. But it was that angel who really inspired it."[81]

Louis B. Mayer was so thrilled with the movie and so anxious about Edna's response that he wrote to her before she even saw it. "I know it will do you, personally, and the Home, a world of good. It will show people in such a lovely way the wonderful work you are doing."[82]

Oh, That Red Hair!

MGM decided to pre-release *Blossoms* in a major metropolitan area far from Texas and selected New York City's famed Radio City Music Hall. It opened on June 26, 1941, and went on to have the hall's biggest Fourth of July weekend in its nine-year history. A successful opening there was the sure sign of a hit movie. Generally, opening movies played at the hall for only a week or so, but *Blossoms* was held over for three weeks.

New York Post reviewer Archer Winsten declared that Radio City Music Hall had "worked itself into a lather" over the film and that Greer Garson's hair was "one of Nature's finest wonders." In fact, that red hair came in for numerous comments from reviewers, including several who first complained that Greer never aged in the thirty-year course of the movie but then added that, on the other hand, it would have been a shame to age that perfect face or put silver in that glorious red hair. Wrote the *San Francisco Chronicle*, "In the person of Greer Garson, Mrs. Edna Gladney…is certainly the most decorative crusader the movies have yet dealt with. Her story would be inspiring enough even without Miss Garson's beautiful red hair." The *Stamford (TX) American* told its readers, "You have never seen anything until you see red-headed Miss Garson holding a red-headed baby in her arms." And Walter Winchell proclaimed her as "the gal Technicolor was invented for."

But the reviewer at the *New Orleans Times-Picayune* worked himself into a lather equal to that of Radio City's. "You've seen dawn on the Grand Canyon, maybe, and moon over Miami, the sunset in *A Star Is Born* and opening night at the Metropolitan Opera, but you haven't seen anything gorgeous until your mortal eyes have beheld Miss Garson in a blue party dress."

Equal praise was lavished on her sensitive portrayal of Edna, and more than one filmgoer and reviewer felt that not only was Garson a shoo-in for an Oscar as Best Actress but also that *Blossoms* would be among the year's

"Ten Best." (It was on many Top Ten lists.) "If she doesn't win the Academy Award," declared Hollywood columnist Louella Parsons, "it's because we will have better motion pictures than we have the right to expect." The *Omaha World Herald* called "Edna's" speech to the Texas legislature "one of those great movie scenes you won't soon forget…The word, 'illegitimate,' by the way, still appears on birth certificates in some states. I'll wager this picture will help complete [Edna's work]."

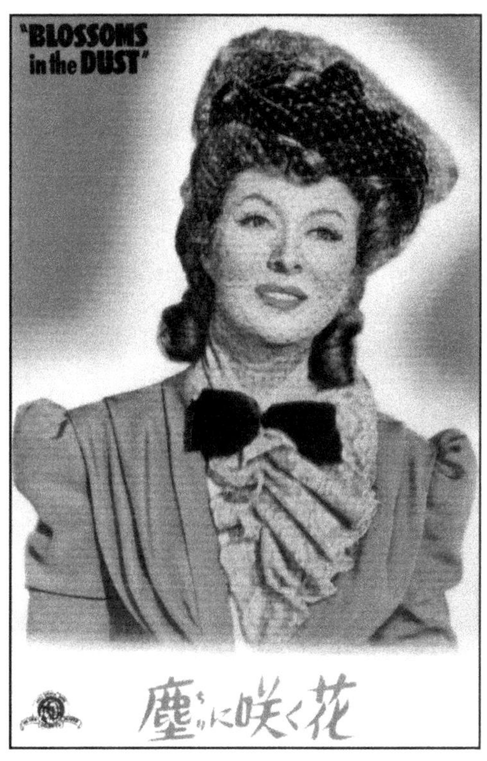

Blossoms in the Dust showed around the world, including Australia, Canada, Great Britain, Italy, Japan, New Zealand and South Africa. *Deb Chester Maclin/Warner Bros. Entertainment.*

Dallas Morning News critic John Rosenfield, in referring to her "illegitimate children" quote in the speech, agreed. "This viewpoint, now implemented in Texas law and in the statutes of many other enlightened states, brought upon her the wrath of the bluenoses. But what matter? It was a liberal triumph." Ralph Wheelwright's 1940 story idea listed states that had already followed Texas's example by that time and changed their birth certificates: California, Delaware, Illinois, Michigan, New Jersey and New York. A dozen other states also had similar legislation pending as he wrote. By the fall of 1943, reported the *Santa Fe New Mexican*, "all but three [states] issue them. Colorado will be one of the last."

Blossoms in the Dust had fulfilled the hopes of many by putting this issue before a major audience and helping to change an uncounted number of lives—bringing thousands of children out of bondage, as one critic expressed it. Edna had no problem with the method. MGM had used her story, she said, because "it is difficult to interest people in statistics and organizations. It is necessary to have a personality."[83]

A Grand Night in Fort Worth

MGM's Dallas publicity representative E.B. Coleman arranged a small, private showing of *Blossoms* at the Fort Worth Club on the same day that it premiered at Radio City Music Hall. A number of TCHAS board members, civic leaders, friends and family attended. Among them was Annie May Ely Weichsel of Dallas but formerly of Sherman, who had worked with Edna to establish the Day Nursery there, the "cradle of Mrs. Gladney's social work."

Coleman was also working on the movie's southwestern premiere in Fort Worth, but the date changed constantly as he tried to accommodate actors' and executives' schedules so they could attend. At one point there was even a benefit planned, to be hosted by Greer Garson, but that had to be canceled. Edna finally contacted the studio and asked that the premiere be done on the regular release schedule. Ralph Wheelwright was very disappointed but wrote to Edna that, because of the war in Europe, "these are fast-moving, strange days" that were adversely affecting the movie industry. "This business, like all others, is hard-pressed. There are so many uncertainties and demands."[84]

Blossoms in the Dust premiered at the Egyptian-themed Worth Theater on Friday, July 17, 1941, before the movie went into general release around the country on July 25. The $1 million Worth was the largest theater in Texas when it opened in 1927. It accommodated nearly 2,500 people and boasted a "refrigerated air system" (air conditioning) that changed the air every three minutes—a lovely asset on a day when the temperature had reached 101.2 degrees.

Groups of TCHAS adoptive families flocked to Fort Worth from Amarillo, Dallas, El Paso and Houston to see "their" story. Others rushed to be the first to buy tickets for the showing in other cities.

A dinner for twenty guests honoring Edna was held at the adjoining Worth Hotel before the screening. There she received congratulatory phone calls from Greer Garson, Walter Pidgeon, Irving Asher, Mervyn LeRoy and Ralph Wheelwright, who were unable to attend because of commitments to other films. Western Union stayed busy all day delivering telegrams from friends and admirers, including Louis B. Mayer: "No human endeavor could be more worthy of tribute than your chosen work and ideals." Irving Asher also telegraphed to say it was his "sincere hope that I may serve to carry on the ideals for which you have striven." And director Mervyn LeRoy thanked her for her gift of inspiration that made *Blossoms* possible.

Walter Pidgeon touched Edna's heart with his telegram. "To have played so fine a role as that of Samuel Gladney was a treasured privilege and it is my sincere hope that those who knew and loved him may again be touched

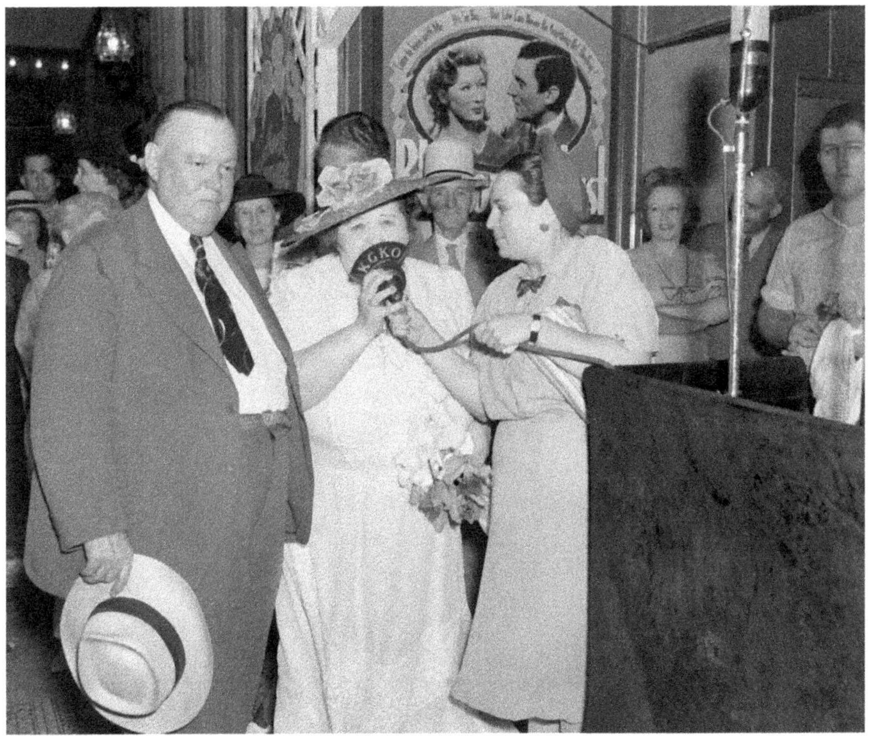

At the premiere, Edna is flanked by Fort Worth mayor I.N. McCrary and newspaperwoman Mary Sears Rhodes. Fort Worth Star-Telegram *Collection, Special Collections, University of Texas–Arlington.*

with his great understanding and kindness." Greer Garson telegraphed that she was thinking of Edna. "You must be very happy. I know I have found great happiness in being merely your screen shadow. It was a joy to be even a reflection of a life so beautifully lived."

Other Hollywood stars—Joan Crawford, Hedy Lamarr, Maureen O'Sullivan and Robert Taylor, among them—also sent congratulations.

Every Gladiola in Texas

In a bow to the movie's signature flower, E.B. Coleman purchased hundreds of pink and white gladioli to decorate the theater—every gladiola in Texas, someone joked. They filled huge vases in the lobby and foyer and were woven into trellises. Friends sent more arrangements, and two charming young ladies handed out rosebuds to all the women present. At 7:15 p.m., one thousand fresh roses were dropped on Seventh Street in front of the theater. KGKO Radio broadcast the festivities, and Fort Worth's Mayor McCrary escorted the heroine of the day to her seat in the theater.

After the show, audience members thronged around Edna to express their best wishes. At the end of the evening, she injected a note of reality when she told everyone, "It is all very wonderful. I am so happy and satisfied, but there still is work to be done."

Everyone was gay, pushing to the backs of their minds for just one night the headlines in that day's *Star-Telegram*: Behind America Was Peace; Ahead Was War…Soviet Union Acknowledged the German Advance Toward Moscow…Plans for Large-scale New Army Camps at Waco, Bastrop and Paris Are Revealed…Government Expects Defense Expenditures of $3,000,000,000 a Month by 1943…and an editorial: U.S. Doesn't Want War and Will Still Not Want It Even as It Fires the First Shots.

The Reviews Are In

Though some reviewers criticized *Blossoms* as overly sentimental and weepy—and more than one wondered what the title meant—most praised the film, particularly for its frank talk and unabashed use of the word "illegitimate." Viewers today might raise a disbelieving eyebrow at the controversy the film caused, but in 1941, this was strong stuff. Industry publication *Variety* reported that some newspapers wouldn't even run the advertisements.

The *Rockland County (NY) Leader* warned, "Timid souls who dislike such forthright dialogue like 'Bad girls don't have babies,' had better stay home. *Blossoms in the Dust* does not pull its punches." The *Cleveland Citizen* added, "You may not agree with the unconventional ideas it sets forth, and call them propaganda, but it will surely set you to thinking. It is a play for moderns and gives old fogies no quarter."

"You'll be surprised and thrilled, I think," wrote Washington, D.C.'s *Daily News* critic, "at how fully Hollywood permits this problem to be stated and how frank are the words with which the embattled reformer argues." Cleveland's always forthright *Plain Dealer* called it "worthy propaganda but it is powerful entertainment first…Perhaps most of you have never heard of Mrs. Gladney…considering her work, ours is a shameful ignorance."

Louella Parsons approved of "the prevalent trend toward glorifying men and women of achievement and fame who are still living...It is definitely a new phase in movie making and opens a vast field for exciting material." The *Miami Herald* reviewer challenged "the best of writers to create a character such as...Edna Gladney," while the respected *Christian Science Monitor* called *Blossoms* "a serious statement on the subject of environment vs. supposed heredity." And more than one paper pointed out the film's timely release "with so many childless homes today being brightened by adopted babies."

Even Texas senator Tom Connally, chairman of the U.S. Senate Foreign Relations Committee, took to the floor to call attention to both Edna's work and the movie industry's willingness to recognize the efforts of Americans who rarely received public acclaim.

Fan Mail from Around the World

Edna received so many letters after *Blossoms* premiered that it took her months to catch up. To friends who had known Sam, Edna expressed her appreciation that the film had glorified him. Without his interest and moral and financial support, "I could not have carried on, for it takes courage." In a few letters, she spoke of her mother as well. "Of course it was Mamma and Mr. Gladney who made it possible for me to accomplish what I have, and you will never know how hard it was for me to sit through that picture when they, the two who helped me most, were not there." And never did she forget to thank "the fine families who have taken these children, loved them, developed and trained them into useful citizens, which is the most satisfying experience that any one could have."

She was pleased to receive congratulations from social work colleagues. Mrs. W.H. Davidson with the Texas Department of Public Health and Welfare wrote, "The production is decidedly a step forward in the picture industry" that enlightened the public and eliminated the confusing ideas that have surrounded adoption. "It is the best example of philanthropy ever expressed in any form," declared Effie Reagor of Ellis County (Texas) Family Welfare. "The picture erases more of the prejudices against the efforts the Welfare Agencies have made to assist the human race." Edna wrote back and assured Reagor that "I shall always be interested in Texas Children, perhaps not as dramatic in [their] appeal as the [European] refugee children but...something must be done."

Personally rewarding to Edna were the letters from young women who aspired to go into social work after seeing *Blossoms in the Dust*. To one California teenager, she advised taking sociology in college. "To be a successful social service worker, one must have much training and a world of patience...I should love to hear from you again in a few years." She wrote to a young Wisconsin woman, "I don't believe you could choose a profession that would give you greater satisfaction in helping others."

Because of the war's disruption, it would take a decade or more for *Blossoms* to open in other countries: Argentina, Australia, Austria, Brazil, Canada, Denmark, Finland, France, Greece, Hungary, Italy, Japan, New Zealand, Norway, Peru, Poland, Portugal, South Africa, Spain, Sweden and the United Kingdom. But not until 1973 did *Bluten im Staub* appear on German television. This international audience brought Edna some interesting letters, a few of which survive in her personal papers.

From South Africa in 1944 came a letter from a man who thought he'd "lived a very presentable life." But after seeing *Blossoms*, he realized that most people "do not live, we merely exist. Life consists in bringing happiness into the lives of others, regardless of what privations the well-doer may suffer...It is your pattern that I am going to follow in my attempt to form a new way of life." An Englishwoman, born illegitimately, wrote in 1947, "If there were more of your kind in the world what a different place it would be!" The family that raised her never let her forget her origin, and "all my life I've lived with this awful shadow."

"Admired Lady, people like you should have eternal youth," wrote a Barcelona fan in 1950, "your work will make your name legend." A Peruvian man echoed those sentiments. Edna's name and her work, he declared, should "be mentioned in the teaching of History, and it should be stressed that there were many great men that were orphans."

A young navy ensign stationed in Seattle was moved to also write a letter that probably reduced Edna to tears. "A fellow doesn't mind devoting his time and, perhaps his life, to a country that stands for all the things good, and all the things humane you have inculcated into our National life...Miss Garson's portrayal... has brought home to me the true picture of Americanism...and though it will cost me a lot of time, a lot of heartaches, and perhaps my life—I thank God I am at last convinced that the cause for which my life may be taken is one of decency, human kindness, tolerance, and Christian charity."

Others told of unhappy situations. In Massachusetts, "the 'Biddies' in charge of State work put the children in some terrible homes without even looking into the past or present or future. They are very cruel."

A friend, Mrs. Charles Batsell, whose son-in-law Dr. Clayton Shirley served on the TCHAS Board, told Edna of the Sherman audiences going to see *Blossoms*. Their "crowd" liked to go to the Texas Theater on Sunday to visit as well as see a movie. "Well, today, it was a strange audience. The house was simply packed & jammed with people standing in [the] lobby long before the first showing was over. But so many [were] strange faces—and then it dawned upon me that these people didn't usually go to the Texas, but they are the people you once helped—helped them or some of their families and friends…I was real touched for I feel it was a tribute to you."

But along with the welcome letters were a few rather strange ones. A Lexington, Kentucky publisher sent her a copy of *Man in Our Image: The Same Man the Eugenicist Would Make* by Scient Auk, which offered "a chaste way for every child born being immaculately conceived and of having the very best ancestry on at least one side"—what would later be probably called test tube babies. They would be perfect for adoption, he assured her.

And Nan Britton of Illinois sent her congratulations on *Blossoms'* "direct and forceful…appeal for the child born out of marriage!...As an unmarried mother, I am grateful to you, and to all others in this country, who are responsible for the steady if slow progress that has been made on behalf of the child born unconventionally…The day is bound to come when not only will these innocent children be regarded as legitimate and registered in all states at birth without the stigmatizing adjective; but they shall be registered correctly as to paternity…and failure to do this shall constitute a criminal offense. Only this drastic—but how right!—requirement by law will put an end to illegitimacy." Britton was the author of *The President's Daughter*, published in 1927, which detailed her affair with future president of the United States Warren G. Harding and declared him the father of her child. She started the Elizabeth Ann League, named for her daughter, to seek legal aid and justice for out-of-wedlock children.

Greer Garson was also deluged with "a great number of letters from legislators, judges and welfare workers in this country with many interesting comments on the situation regarding birth certificates in various states and many letters, too, that would touch your kind heart from men and women who started life under the handicap that you have done so much to remove." Garson played her part on screen so well, in fact, that she also received hundreds of letters from people wishing to adopt a child from her. She had to tell them she was Mrs. Gladney on screen only.[85]

"NOBODY'S CHILDREN"

Just three days after the Fort Worth premiere, star Greer Garson and director Mervyn LeRoy took part in a radio program, *Nobody's Children*, which was hosted by Walter White and broadcast from the Children's Home Society of California. The show, which ran from 1939 to 1942, was created by White when he and his wife were told, erroneously, that they could not have children and so began touring orphanages. Hollywood celebrities brought attention to the program and the needs of homeless children "in the hope that nobody's children, everywhere, might become somebody's children."

White was elated with *Blossoms in the Dust*, the first movie, in his opinion, to intelligently present adoption. The broadcast began on a light note as White asked Greer what she and Edna had discussed when the latter came to dinner at her house: clothes and hairdos? "I should say not," replied the actress. "We talked about babies!" LeRoy added, "Mrs. Gladney says that is all she knows—baby talk!"[86] The three agreed that too many Americans knew too

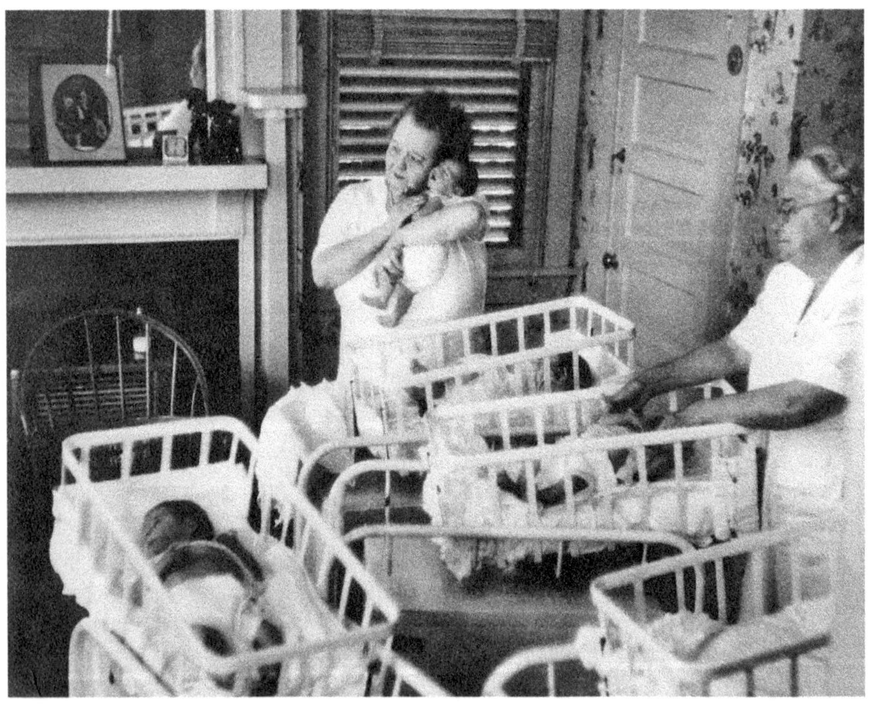

This photo of Edna in the Baby Home nursery appeared in the January 1954 issue of *Woman's Home Companion. Author's collection.*

little about adoption and the complexities of matching parents and child, which White declared to be "the deciding factor of successful adoptions." And he concluded with this heartfelt comment: "Let us hope that the day is not too far distant when every state in this great union will cease to make a bad child of a good and innocent child by branding it illegitimate."

Money and Dresser Drawers

Edna had hoped that *Blossoms, Nobody's Children* and all the attendant publicity would bring in sufficient money to help with the Home's indebtedness. But she soon discovered, as had Father Flanagan at Boys' Town, that the public assumed Metro-Goldwyn-Mayer had paid both institutions major dollars: donations dropped through the floor.

As Pearl Harbor was bombed and the United States declared war on Japan, Edna counted Christmas 1941 gifts. They came to only $2,400—little more than $38,000 today—though some of the gifts were from interesting sources. The last survivor of World War I's Forty-second Division, the famed Rainbow Division composed of National Guard units from twenty-six states and the District of Columbia, sent $100 in gratitude for the two children he'd received from the Texas Children's Home. And a woman also sent $100, saying her husband had enough ties for Christmas.

The problem was that, thanks to *Blossoms, Nobody's Children* and all that publicity, the El Paso Street facility was full of babies, so many of them that Edna and the staff were forced to use dresser drawers as cribs. The Texas Department of Public Welfare sent social workers to help process the number of applicants both bringing in and wanting to adopt babies.

And the war had only just begun.

Chapter 8

"War Babies Are Coming in Very Fast"

Greer Garson, Ralph Wheelwright and other correspondents kept Edna up to date with the war's effect on Hollywood and the movie industry as Pearl Harbor and the fear of Japanese invasion galvanized the West Coast.

"That Nasty Man with the Mustache"

Prime international movie markets had been shut down one by one as Hitler—Irving Asher dubbed him "that nasty man with the mustache"—advanced across Europe. This delayed the release of *Blossoms in the Dust* for years and even decades in some instances and reduced the amount of money it brought in. (MGM would rerelease it and other wartime movies in the 1950s in an effort to recoup more of its expenses.) Edna's story had cost at least $1 million because of the use of Technicolor. "Had it not been made so beautifully," Ralph Wheelwright explained to her, "*Blossoms* may have shown a profit. But with the cost so high, it fell far short of meeting the original negative cost."[87]

MGM had been expecting ticket sales that at least equaled 1938's *Boys Town*. Thanks to that film's box-office bonanza, the studio had been able to help Father Flanagan by donating $250,000 to build a new dormitory when gifts dried up after the release of the movie. Boys Town, like the TCHAS, was flooded with applicants after all the movie publicity. And while the studio had purchased the first film's story rights for only $5,000, it paid a whopping $100,000 for the rights to the Boys Town sequel, which did poorly in theaters compared to its predecessor.

Hollywood itself was given over increasingly to military morale and training film projects. "California," Greer Garson wrote to Edna a week after Pearl Harbor, "is humming with defense program activity. Let's hope it won't be humming to a more disastrous tune any of these starry nights. However, everybody is steadfast and cheerful and busy. I think we have all come to believe that Providence will either send good fortune or, if misfortune comes, will send strength to withstand it."

Ralph told Edna of the "very depressing" blackouts in Los Angeles, where black cloths or shades covered every window. His wife, Phinie Louise, had joined the Woman's Ambulance Corps, which drilled two nights every week. "Thousands upon thousands of soldiers are everywhere," he continued, including a regiment stationed at MGM. "Our beaches are studded with artillery. Our skies are roaring with planes, day and night."

The situation quickly worsened. "Like every other business that is not making guns and planes, we are quite harassed and hardly know what is coming next," Ralph wrote in March 1942. "Right now, we are wondering where film is coming from, let alone actors. We can get along without the actors, perhaps, but not film…Stars no longer have days or weeks off. We have a Victory Committee which operates under Government advice for the purpose of supplying shows and appearances in the Army and Navy camps…Some of the shows are even being sent out of the country to distant places." He described the "thunder of aircraft guns, blazing just over the hills…Spring is here, the flowers are blooming, but it doesn't seem the same world."

Edna kept the first Christmas of the war as she had always done, sending gifts to many of her adoptees. According to *Fort Worth Star-Telegram* columnist Edith Alderman Guedry, Edna, "a lover of beauty herself…does much to spread beauty after they leave her home." To thirty children "who had come under her roof and who were not adoptable and are now in various state institutions," she sent two books, one on American presidents and one on bells, wrapped in red, white and blue. Tucked inside each was a small American flag and a dollar bill. "With them went a personal note from [Edna] herself, saying 'I want you to know what magnificent children you are and that you are 100 per cent American citizens.'"

"To dozens upon dozens of older children," Guedry continued, "Mrs. Gladney sent personal messages, warm, motherly messages penned in her own hand. Before the holiday season is over—and for Mrs. Gladney [it] will not be over until way into January—she will pen close to a thousand personal messages. Each basketload of mail that has come in will be answered by her, not dictated."[88]

"In War or Peace"

As more and more young men went off to military camps, some stopped in Fort Worth to say hello to their "Aunt Edna," as the children she'd placed—and everyone else—affectionately called her. It was most gratifying, she told a reporter. "Shortly after we entered the war…when youth were being drafted in great numbers, time and again young men for whom I had found homes years before came to me before they left for training and thanked me for finding them such wonderful parents. Repeatedly they said that their parents couldn't possibly have been better if they had really been their own."[89]

The organization's newest brochure featured a baby on the cover, surrounded by stars and with an American flag flying over him. "In War or Peace," it proclaimed, the Texas Children's Home was the "Greatest Charity of All." Inside, Edna declared, "We are fighting again for human freedom and especially for the future of our children in a free world…Children must be safeguarded—and they can be safeguarded—in the midst of this total war." A photo of a diaper bore the logo "Our Only Badge Is a Safety Pin and Service."

Edna grappled with several problems in making placements. Older children were now quite difficult to place even though they "are very interesting, starved for affection and always want to belong to some one. Older couples would find life very worthwhile and give themselves an excuse for living, to take children…One interesting gentleman wrote wanting an older child. We sent history and pictures of a fourteen year old boy. The man was so impressed he wrote the most beautiful letter I have ever read in my life, offering this boy his home, his love and his name. The boy was placed there, made splendid grades and has been accepted by [the father's] family and all their friends as this man's heir."[90]

Another difficulty lay with the Fort Worth Community Chest, which restricted TCHAS placements to within a radius of 250 miles of Fort Worth and required Edna to accept children only from surrounding counties. A good number of the children came from this region, and placing them in the same area violated policies the Home had long followed. Both Reverend I.Z.T. Morris and Edna believed a child should be placed far from his or her original family to avoid interference by blood relatives and to give both them and the birth mothers a fresh start. "We have placed children from Shanghai, China to Corsicana, Texas and in every state of the union," Edna pointed out, but to no avail.

She regularly complained to Ralph about this interference and finally grew so frustrated that she wrote to Louis B. Mayer, whom she'd named an honorary vice-president on the board of directors. He had shown such interest in her work that she was asking his advice "as to whether I should try to continue this social work." Seven thousand couples were now on the waiting list, "and the majority of my [adoptive] parents are now ready for their second, third and fourth child." The Community Chest, she continued, had disregarded the Home's excellent record, more interested in the costs of placement than a proper placement.

The TCHAS, Edna grumbled, had received $7,000 in 1941 (about $111,370 today) "and then [they] claimed I couldn't stay within my budget. The fact is, I've never had a budget sufficient to conduct the organization's work." Even though she placed 100 to 150 children each year, from infants to age fourteen, she operated the office with only one secretary and did all the travel and placements herself. "And with the additional service demands coming to us within the last several months, all of which we are supremely happy to work out, we are facing the ultimate crisis of this organization. In short, the lack of financing is paralyzing [us]."

Without a permanent endowment, she continued, "it seems rather too apparent that we must close our doors, our hearts, our minds, our souls—to the constant need and pleas of these mothers, babies, and the fine young couples who so desperately want and need these children. If there is any other alternative I have been unable to discover it…I have fought this situation and problem," Edna concluded, "until now I'm afraid I must admit defeat."[91]

Desperate, indeed, she must have been to write such a letter. It should be noted, however, that she was not only aware of the financial arrangements made for Boys Town but that she kept in her personal papers a news clipping showing Mayer's annual salary to be in excess of $600,000 (more than $9 million today).

Mayer was most likely staggered at her letter, considering, as he wrote her, that "I am really not familiar with charity organization." But, impressed by her life's work, he did her the courtesy of trying to answer as best he could…even if it did sound condescending.

"You ask whether or not you should carry on in the face of discouragement. I don't think you need to ask that question, for you have answered it yourself in the years of struggle and sacrifice, in your courageous fight against misunderstanding and criticism. Of course you will have troubles. You will always have to fight, but you will always carry on, I am sure. That is why you are Edna Gladney…you must be bountifully blessed for the happiness you have brought into so many hundreds of lives…Yes, Edna Gladney, I am sure you will go on."

Mayer then went on to douse any hopes Edna might have had of assistance from MGM.

"We are very happy that *Blossoms in the Dust* brought inspiration to so many people. It is unfortunate that the picture did not enjoy the financial success it deserved. That it served a fine humanitarian cause, however, is deeply gratifying."[92]

Still Going Hollywood

The entertainment industry continued to play a part in Edna's life and the life of the TCHAS. Comic actor Clem Bevans, who specialized in "old coot" roles in such films as *Tall in the Saddle*, *Sergeant York* and *The Yearling*, adopted a daughter from Edna after sixteen years of marriage and little hope of having a child.

There was also some discussion about Edna helping Joan Crawford—a San Antonio, Texas native—when the actress was forced to return her son, adopted through a baby broker, to his birth mother. (She had found out the adoptive mother was a movie star.) Considering these events, columnist Louella Parsons cautioned her readers. "Hollywood stars who have adopted children and obtained them through the Cradle, Mrs. Edna Gladney or any church orphanage, have nothing to worry about. No organization of this type would dream of telling the real parents the names of the adopted parents. That's always part of the bargain." Actress Ann Sothern had an experience similar to Crawford's, but Parsons also listed actors with successful adoptions: George Burns and Gracie Allen, Jack Benny, Pat O'Brien, Bob Hope and Irene Dunne.[93]

Greer Garson and Walter Pidgeon reprised their *Blossoms* roles on Cecil B. DeMille's *Lux Radio Theater* on February 16, 1942. Edna listened to the broadcast from the Saint Anthony Hotel in San Antonio, where she was on vacation with Fort Worth friend Ethel Burton.

Garson went on to star in the comedy-drama *When Ladies Meet* opposite Joan Crawford, while Pidgeon was filming the classic *How Green Was My Valley*, which beat out *Blossoms* for Best Picture in 1942. There had been high hopes for *Blossoms* at the Academy Awards, but Greer also lost (to Joan Fontaine in *Suspicion*) and cinematographers Karl Freund and W. Howard Greene lost to *Blood and Sand*. Only the art department—Cedric Gibbons, Urie McCleary and Edwin B. Willis—carried home statuettes that night for Best Art Direction/Interior Decoration/Color in *Blossoms*.

When MGM announced it would star Greer Garson in *Mrs. Miniver*, fans who had seen her and Pidgeon in *Blossoms* lobbied for them to be together again. In all, this golden couple made eight movies: *Blossoms in the Dust*, *Mrs. Miniver*, *Madame Curie*, *Mrs. Parkington*, *Julia Misbehaves*, *That Forsyte Woman*, *The Miniver Story* and *Scandal at Scourie*.

Ralph Wheelwright continued to keep Edna apprised of summertime war conditions in Los Angeles. Most beaches were unavailable, with "guns and barbed wire all over them…[and they] are too far away for tires unless you want to spend the day." Ralph had joined a volunteer fire department, rough work in the canyon area where he then lived. To her delight, he also attached the results of a poll made by Radio City Music Hall of New York moviegoers' choices of the ten best movies: *Blossoms* was number ten.[94]

In November, an elated Ralph wrote to tell Edna that Phinie Louise was pregnant; little Phinie was indignant that the new baby wasn't coming from Mrs. Gladney, as she had. He ruefully told her that their recent trip to the beach house was likely to be their last for some time. "It was totally blacked out every night, with gunfire all day long from the forts and ships at sea. Up our way we have been dimmed out to almost total darkness and driving at night is very hazardous. With gas rationing we won't be able to drive anyway. I don't know how we will get to work." Ralph had gotten his draft card, too. "They are taking married men right and left out here. It's only a question of time…we have been unable to buy bacon or ham for weeks…[little] Phinie Louise is irate about the chewing gum situation…Right now things do not look so very good [at MGM]."[95]

Needing Her Help

The war news was almost overwhelming. The United States took back Guadalcanal from Japan at a high cost and, with the Allies, invaded North

Africa. The Soviets and Nazis were locked in the Battle of Stalingrad. And the first word of Nazi atrocities against Jews began to come out of Europe.

Edna's Christmas 1942 appeal letter was short and blunt. "War babies are coming in very fast…We are in debt…we can't wish you a Merry Christmas this year." The Home's board president from 1939 to March 1942, Captain John W. Herbert, was killed in aerial combat over the jungles of New Guinea in the fall of 1942, but the news did not arrive in Fort Worth until early 1943. And Amon G. Carter Jr., son of the longtime benefactor and grandson of Edna's close friend Ethel Burton, would soon be captured in North Africa and held as a prisoner of war in Poland for more than two years.

With husbands and fathers dead or in prison camps and birth fathers who never returned to marry and care for their children, some women—both married and single—struggled so desperately to make ends meet that they were forced to give their children to others. In the summer of 1942, the *Dallas Morning News* had reported that birth rates were rising sharply for both legitimate and illegitimate babies. Social agencies did not have enough staff to care for the young women leaving their rural homes in great numbers, coming to boomtowns and "getting into trouble."[96] A year later, the situation had not improved.

It was a litany of woe and an enormous workload for Edna. Everything was in short supply, from diapers to clothes to food to nurses, many of whom had gone into military service. Babies had to be placed sooner, and hospital stays for birth mothers shortened. Most of the babies were delivered at the West Texas Maternity Hospital in south Fort Worth. From there, they were picked up when only one or two days old and taken to the Baby Home to be placed out.

Edna was also in demand outside the TCHAS as other state legislatures continued to take up the birth certificate controversy. Since *Blossoms in the Dust*, she had received many letters from both organizations and individuals, asking for her help, sure that her presence and her testimony would sway any opposition. An old friend from her Cuba days, Dr. Jack W. Amesse of Denver, also wrote that Colorado would shortly be considering a bill providing for the adoption of children with unmarried mothers, the legitimization of the birth and issuing second birth certificates. The Denver Chamber of Commerce, he told Edna, had arranged for a special showing of *Blossoms* before the vote. Could she come and address the group? "We feel your personal attendance would do more to crystallize popular opinion than any other endeavor conceivable."[97]

Edna had to decline for health reasons, but she assured Amesse that "you will never regret any time, money or interest you may give…this subject."

She also wrote of her recent request to Colorado for the birth certificate of a legitimate adopted child, but the state had refused to issue a new one showing the adopted parents.

In early May 1943, Ralph wrote to Edna—"mother of none, and yet of so very many"—that he had a son, Ralph Jr. "We know now, that there is no difference in adoption and natural parenthood. We feel the same [for both Phinie and Ralph]." He ended with a sentiment every adoptive parent holds dear. "A child is your child, it matters not at all how that child reaches your home. The way to your heart is the same." A few months later, he wrote similarly. "Both were born in our hearts. They simply came to us by different paths God destined."[98]

Edna and Greer Garson met on Texas soil for the first time when the actress stopped in Fort Worth to perform with the Hollywood Cavalcade at the Will Rogers Memorial Coliseum; she spoke warmly of Edna's work at this war bond rally. Greer said that visiting 1315 West El Paso Street was "like coming home." During their very brief visit, she told Edna that her mother received regular letters from European friends who had seen *Blossoms*.[99]

Edna's joy at seeing her screen counterpart was dimmed by a painful personal loss. Her aunt Flora Goetz, who had welcomed her in 1904 when she came to Fort Worth, died in July. And in 1944, she would lose both Florence and Arthur, too, barely five months apart. A large part of her Fort Worth family was gone.

And as the second full year of the war wound down, Edna sent out her annual appeal for funds. "This is the second war that we have witnessed, and served war babies, but whether it is war times or peace times, we have rendered the same service of accepting nameless, homeless and deserted babies for more than forty years. Over six thousand children have been accepted by us, and adopted, and now have very important places in civilian life as well as in our armed forces." In her letter, she hesitates to tell these friends to whom she's writing of the organization's bleak finances since they all have demands, too. But if they can help, it will mean continuing the Home's work without interruption.

> *No one could wish you a Merry Christmas in the midst of all this conflict—I do wish you good health, long life, continued courage to do your daily tasks, and spiritual guidance from above and constantly renewed, and, may I add, that you will never be too busy or too important to hear and know the cries and needs of all little, unprotected children, is the wish of Edna Gladney, State Superintendent.*

Chapter 9

TRAVELS WITH AUNT EDNA

In 1942, the Baby Home was enlivened by the arrival of Edna's cousin Mary Owen of Milwaukee. After not seeing each other for many years, the two happened to meet again at Dallas's Adolphus Hotel, where Mary's sister, Virginia, was modeling for Neiman-Marcus. Edna invited the young women to visit her in Fort Worth, which they did, but Mary decided to stay on and help out, moved by admiration of Edna's great work. She lived and worked there for four years and, in a recent series of phone and personal interviews, has shared a treasure-trove of stories with the author about her Aunt Edna.

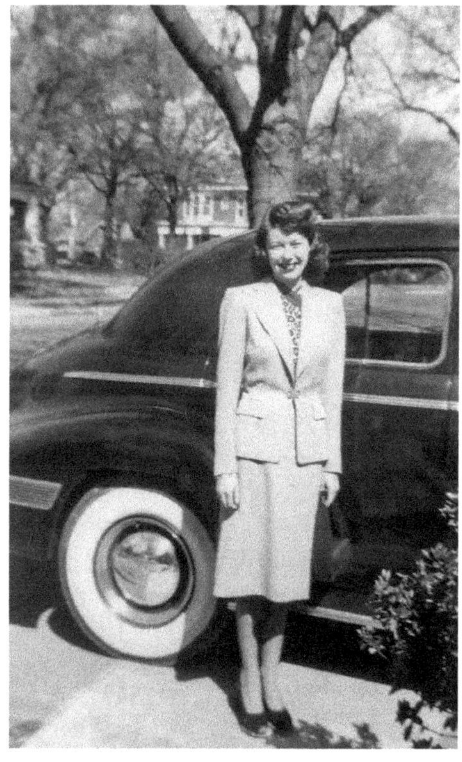

Mary Owen, Edna's cousin from Milwaukee, lived and worked at the Baby Home from 1942 to 1946. *Deb Chester Maclin.*

"And Where Would That Be?"

Edna Gladney was an amazing woman, but driving was not one of her talents, as anyone who ever rode with her would tell you. Her legs were too short to reach the pedals, so she held her cane in her right hand to push them and steered with her left. At some point, horrified adoptive parents rode with her, discovered this and outfitted her car with hand-operated pedals. Edna was also notorious for going her own way—in every way. One stunned Fort Worth policeman watched her back down a one-way street…the wrong way. "Lady," he said, "what you did isn't even on my list [of offenses]!" He let her off with a warning.

But then came the day she did get a ticket and had to appear in court. Of course, the judge knew her, as did most Fort Worth judges, through her work with the Home. When the policeman read the charge, the judge just looked at him. "My dear little Mrs. Gladney would never do anything like that," he told the officer. "You must have made a mistake." The case was dismissed.

So Mary drove when she and Edna traveled to visit placements, do home studies or just go to one of their favorite Mexican restaurants, Joe's, as they called it—the now internationally known Joe T. Garcia's—and, of course, everyone there knew Edna, too. She had found the ideal traveling companion in Mary and often joked that when the younger woman said she was homesick, she meant she was sick of home and ready to hit the road. On one occasion, Mary suggested they go somewhere for vacation where no one knew Edna Gladney. Still embroiled in all the publicity surrounding *Blossoms in the Dust*, Edna put her hands on her hips, asking simply, "And where would that be?"

Mary was always amazed, and frequently appalled, at what Edna would do. On one trip, somewhere near Natchez, Mississippi, the pair passed a gated estate with beautiful gardens and a large "No Trespassing" sign. Edna told Mary to pull in so she could see the flowers—her passion—but Mary was horrified. "You can't just go in there!" But she obeyed, and when the owner came out, Edna greeted him with her signature charm. She introduced herself and Mary and told him she just had to see his lovely gardens. Not only did he give them a tour, but he and his wife also invited the travelers in for tea afterward.

In Colorado, accompanied by the Baby Home's African American cook, Ida Mae, the pair stayed in a house belonging to adoptive parents. The living room had a beautiful view of the Rocky Mountains, but all the furniture faced away from it. So at Edna's instigation, the three rearranged the room.

When time came to leave, Mary asked if they shouldn't put it all back in place. "Why should we? They should have known better than to hide the view!" Ida Mae traveled with them several times on vacation, including to the Grand Canyon, where Edna, without fanfare, had her eat with them in the main dining room. In other, more racially restrictive areas, they would bring her food to the car.

The two once stayed at the famous Broadmoor Hotel in Colorado Springs, where a doctors' convention was also meeting. One physician recognized Edna from *Blossoms* publicity and, concerned about her weight and a possible heart attack, cautioned Mary not to take her up Pike's Peak with its breathtaking—literally—height of 14,114 feet above sea level. Too late, Mary replied; they'd already been. The doctor was dumbfounded at Edna's audacity.

Once, Edna took a notion to stop along the way to their western destination and visit her cousin, Frank Lloyd Wright, at his Arizona residence, Taliesin West. Mary asked if they shouldn't call first, but Edna wanted to just drop in. "We can't just go into his house!" "Yes, we can," and they did, even though Wright was not there. Edna believed firmly that owners would be delighted at her interest in their beautiful homes. And nine times out of ten, Mary laughed, they were because her personality was so overwhelming.

Their business travels often took them to small towns with minimal accommodations. In one seedy East Texas hotel, they entered their room, and Edna said, "Now, I'm going to show you a trick." She turned off the lights, flipped back the bed covers, then quickly turned the lights back on to see if there were bedbugs in the linens. "No, this one's okay."

At Home and Work with Edna

Exhausted by war demands and lack of supplies, staff and sleep, Edna was relieved to have Mary working there and put her in charge of interviewing the young birth mothers since they were so much closer to her in age. Many nights, with the shortage of nurses, the two also had to feed the babies after a long day's work. And despite her very lean budget, Edna somehow found the time and funds to remodel the Baby Home in 1944 to comply with state health and safety requirements.

On business trips, she and Mary were sometimes accompanied by Edna's niece, Jane Dumas, then a teenager, who helped with the driving while Edna relaxed or slept. The summer 1944 trip was "grand and glorious…and [I] saw over two hundred of my babies…the trip almost killed me but it was worth it."[100]

That was the year she was diagnosed with diabetes; by Christmas, she was proud to tell people she'd lost thirty pounds. ("I must diet and rest, two things I am allergic to.") Edna had very dainty table manners and put only small portions on her plate. But like an alcoholic, she ate in secret, being particularly fond of sweets and fried foods. Her doctor's diagnosis meant she

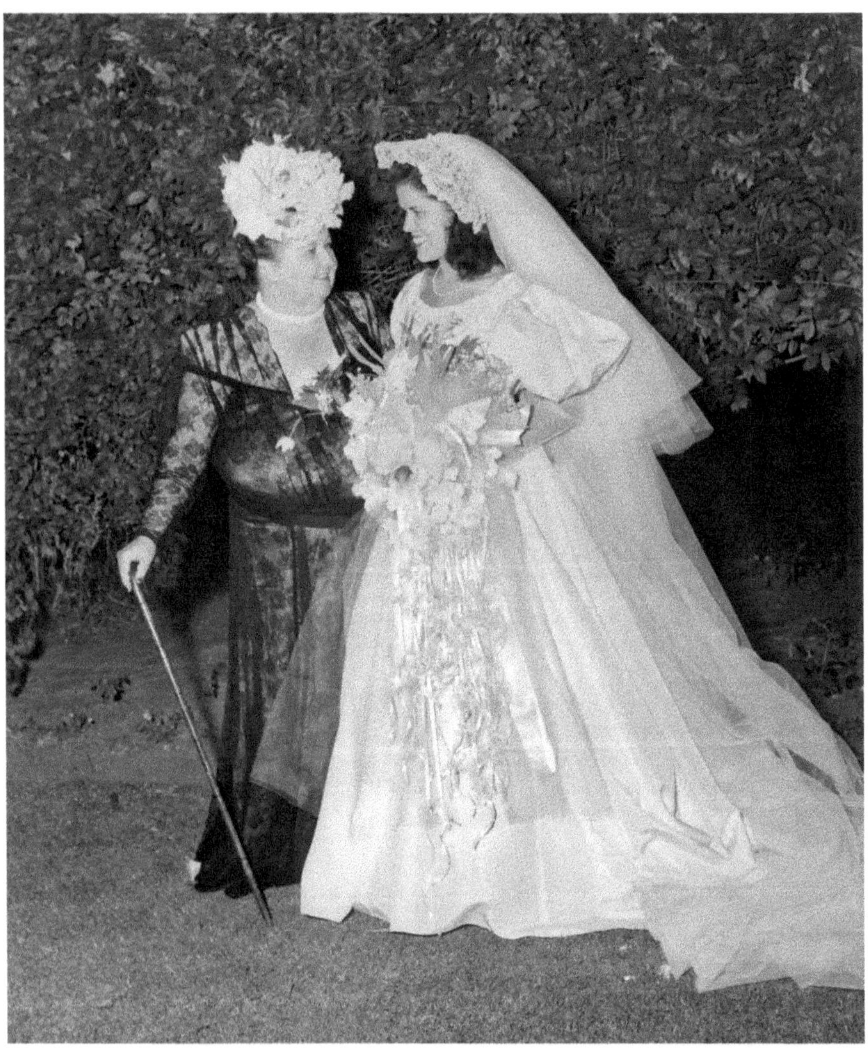

Edna with niece Jane Dumas at her 1947 wedding to Dr. Earl Chester. *Deb Chester Maclin.*

now had to take insulin shots. Giving them to her was one of the few things Mary balked at, and it fell to Ida Mae or one of the nurses.

Despite her weight, Edna was known for her fashionable clothes and especially for her hats, often embellished with silk flowers; many of them were made for her by Margaret Sammer, a friend and head milliner at one of Fort Worth's large department stores. Edna was always meticulous, neat and perfectly put together.

She received many compliments on her peaches-and-cream skin. "Well, I have a lot of it!" she joked. She cleaned her face and neck every day with rubbing alcohol and covered it during the day with alabaster powder. Edna disguised thin lips with lipstick and had to pencil in eyebrows because her own were so sparse.

"I laughed with Aunt Edna until I cried," Mary recalled, quickly adding that she never ridiculed or made fun of anyone except herself. Edna liked to tell the story of visiting a ranch where the owner asked if she'd like to ride. "Poor horse, I'd kill him!"

Edna would go anywhere to help her children and her birth mothers. "She used to drag me places you wouldn't believe," said Mary. "I was always amazed at what she was going to do." And she would enlist anyone she thought could help her. Friends and relatives were accustomed to receiving calls from her, asking them to check out a place or person.

She also took care of her staff and considered them family. When one lost her house in a Trinity River flood, Edna was there with money and supplies. Another night, she received a phone call that Fort Worth police had picked up Robert, the Baby Home's "very sweet and gentle" African American driver and handyman, for vagrancy. He'd insisted on calling Edna, but no one believed he actually knew her. As Mary described it, Edna charged downtown to get him out. "And the minute they heard her name, everyone started quaking in their boots." Edna Gladney took few prisoners.

Peace Time

The war years changed adoption trends in the United States. Younger couples unable to have a pregnancy wanted to wait until the fighting was over to adopt, while older ones desired babies sooner; increasingly, they all wanted boys rather than girls. Between 1937 and 1945, the number of adoptions in the United States tripled. Within the next decade, it astonishingly doubled. Adoption agencies like the TCHAS were inundated with applications, with anywhere from ten to twenty couples waiting for each baby. Social welfare and other agencies that helped unmarried mothers also allowed more of them to keep their children, decreasing the numbers of babies for placing out.

The demand for adoption was so great that this shortage of available infants and youngsters inevitably led to a very busy black market. The *Dallas Morning News* reported that babies sold for as much as $2,000 (about $26,000 today), and most of them were illegitimate.[101] Few states had laws to regulate this traffic.

One advantage of all the publicity and books and movies about unwed mothers and adoptions was the abandonment of fewer babies since scared young women now knew where to go. In the summer of 1945, the *Dallas Morning News* interviewed the staff of Hope Cottage, an adoption agency more than twenty years old and then filled with illegitimate infants. "In the

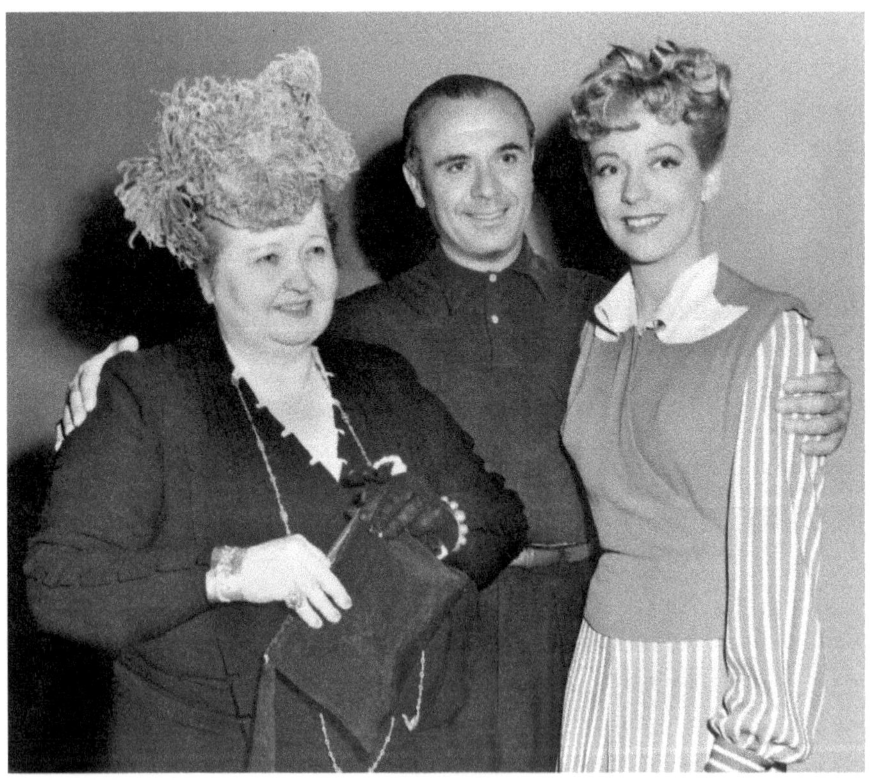

Edna on the MGM set of 1945's *Anchors Aweigh* with her actress cousin Pamela Britton and conductor/pianist Jose Iturbi. *Deb Chester Maclin/Warner Bros. Entertainment.*

past two years, only two foundlings [abandonments] have been brought to Hope Cottage…They used to find them dumped in trashcans, left on doorsteps and in automobiles. Eighteen years ago [when such abandonments were much more common] a baby was rescued from an ant bed two blocks from Hope Cottage after a night and half a day that almost took its life."

In 1947, the *News* carried another article on this troubling subject: of the 100,000 illegitimate babies born that year in the United States, one-third had been, or would be, placed for adoption by black marketers. "The big drawback to black market adoptions, aside from the profiteering angle, is the fact that the [adoptive] parents have no assurance of the fitness of the child they take…[In] an institution…thorough [tests] are made…Those who are impatient resort to the black market, sometimes with tragic results. Those who make casual adoptions take long chances."[102]

Edna would spend years fighting both black and gray market wars, the latter being adoptions made generally through private doctors or attorneys. Among her victories was Texas House Bill 15, passed in June 1949, which prohibited the placement of children for adoption by persons or agencies not licensed by the State Department of Public Welfare; it was intended specifically to target placements by doctors, attorneys or other third parties.

One battle that she did stop fighting in 1946 was with the Fort Worth Community Chest. After years of aggravation, she removed the Texas Children's Home as a member agency when the Chest informed her she could send out only one appeal letter a year and that she could solicit adoptive parents only after their child had been legally adopted for a year. "I'm not taking another cent from them," she exclaimed to Mary Owen. "They try to pauperize you by only letting you take money from them."

Chapter 10

"ANGEL OF MERCY"

After the war, Edna began a serious push to expand the Baby Home's maternity and prenatal care services. The first step was to acquire the medical facilities necessary to satisfy state requirements.

Fortunately, she already knew a place.

MR. STAMPS'S HOSPITAL

In 1934, former West Texas banker Mark S. Stamps built a thirty-five-bed maternity hospital at 2306 Hemphill in south Fort Worth. Stamps recommended that his patients who needed adoption services should place their babies with the TCHAS. The El Paso Street facility, which had a small hospital unit, regularly sent someone the short distance to the maternity hospital to pick up newborns and bring them back. Soon, the two were functioning almost as a unit, though neither had control over the other.

In the early spring of 1947, Stamps leased and transferred all his assets other than the building and real estate to the Home: more than $8,000 in cash (approximately $85,000 today), a 1946 Buick station wagon, hospital equipment, supplies and furnishings. He also rented the building to the organization for $175 a month and remained as superintendent.

The next year, Stamps underwent major surgery and temporarily turned hospital administration over to Edna and the board while he recovered and

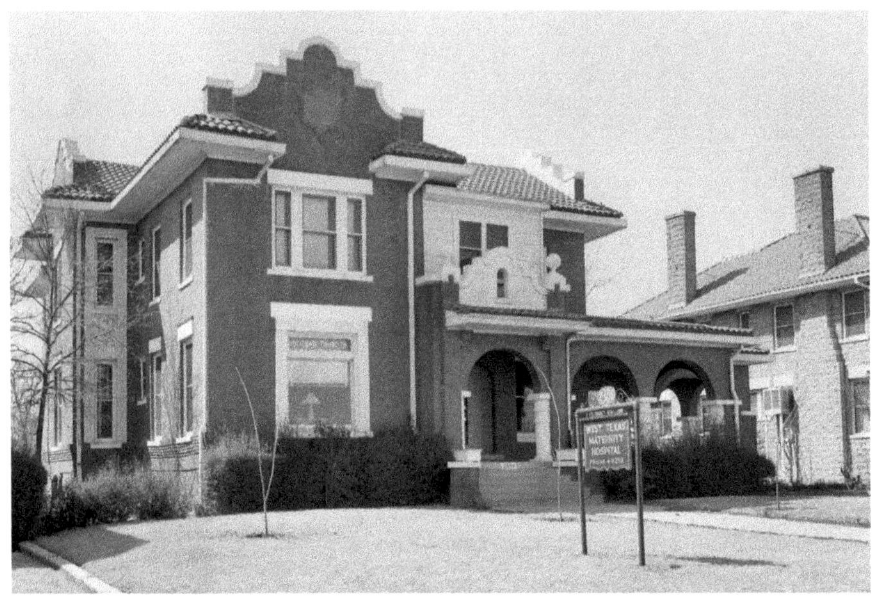

In June 1948, the Home began operating West Texas Maternity Hospital, established in 1934. Fort Worth Star-Telegram *Collection, Special Collections, University of Texas–Arlington.*

mulled selling the facility, which faced bankruptcy. Edna wasted no time alerting her board to this opportunity: a good maternity home required a hospital. The TCHAS charter did not provide for such an operation and had to be amended to include the hospital with its dormitory space for expectant mothers.[103]

Star-Telegram columnist Edith Alderman Deen described it as "a homey red brick two-story house and adjoining frame annex, with a big yard in back." Edna's interior design friend Frances Smith, who also worked on the El Paso Street building, tastefully redecorated it in a green color scheme with Chinese influences. The young women who lived there came from all over the United States and, despite their depression and fears upon arrival, found themselves part of a family.[104] They cooked their own meals, following healthy guidelines, and had educational programs to help them reestablish their lives after leaving. Newborns were immediately transferred to the Baby Home to be examined and cared for by a pediatrician and three nurses until placed.

Edna was known for her rapport with the birth mothers and spent many hours with them, "offering them solace and understanding and helping them to see the brighter side of their situation with her disarming sense of humor."[105] They often had no money or job, were away from home and desperately afraid—all of which they had to endure for months until their babies were born. "It takes all of the love, understanding, tact and courage the staff can command," Edna wrote in her Christmas 1948 letter, "to redirect these sad and precious lives into useful women." She closed with this appeal. "We all have more than we need, and all we have left when we leave this world are the gifts we gave away."

Soon after taking over the hospital, Edna tried to convince her all-male board of directors that she now needed $18,000—about $161,000 today—for a recreation building and laundry. They said no. Edna preferred to achieve her goals with charm but wasn't above using tears and even, when the occasion warranted, a good tongue-lashing. What happened next was related by Eleanor Harris in the January 1954 issue of *Woman's Home Companion*:

> *Rising in wrath, she faced the assembled group of successful businessmen and scolded them as if they were children…"I just wish that all of you men were pregnant!" she told them fiercely. "I wish that you had to wear barrel-like clothes over your misshapen figures. I wish that you had to live like this for nine long months—among strangers. Then I wish that you had your babies…and had to give them up for adoption. You'd give me that recreation building soon enough!"*

It should come as no surprise to hear that they did, though it took several years to complete.[106]

An Endowment at Last

For some time, Edna had advocated for a permanent endowment so she would no longer have to beg for money to make up annual deficits. TCHAS received no support from the state or the Community Chest. Adoptive parents paid part of the costs of their birth mother's residency and delivery: every remaining dollar had to be raised.

Edna was now sixty-two years old and wondering who would replace her, though she assured her donors and parents that she would carry on as long as her body and faculties permitted. (She continued for another twelve years.) At her request, the board established an endowment trust fund, the income from which would go to operations. The initial response was discouraging, and in December 1948, adoptive parents in Houston founded the Edna Gladney Foundation to raise money for operations and endowment. But it would take a group of women determined to help Aunt Edna to really jump-start matters.

In the spring of 1952, the Home's Houston-area adoptive mothers organized an auxiliary to the foundation, the first of what would be many. And since that year marked Edna's twenty-fifth anniversary as superintendent of the TCHAS, the ladies decided to throw a Texas-sized party on November 5 in the Emerald Room of Houston's already legendary Shamrock Hotel—the inspiration for the Conquistador in the film *Giant*. Television and film stars, including Joan Bennett and Zachary Scott, who were performing in a nearby theater, staged a floor show and added even more glamour to the evening. More than eight hundred people filled the elegant room, eager to greet Edna and tell her the latest about their "Gladney babies." Greer Garson and Walter Pidgeon telegraphed congratulations, and the auxiliary presented Edna with a platinum ring set with five diamonds and a sable throw.

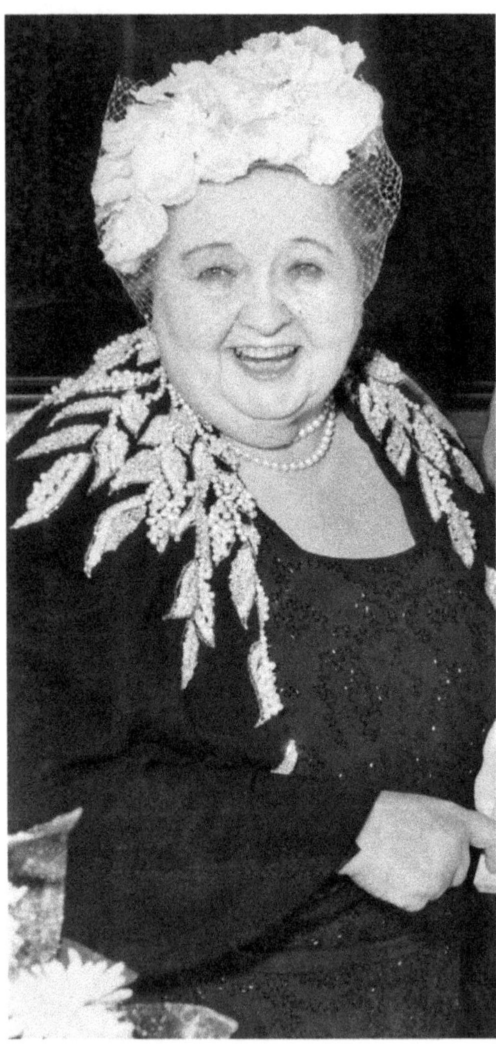

A fashionable Edna in 1959. Fort Worth Star-Telegram *Collection, Special Collections, University of Texas–Arlington.*

Edna tried to speak but was too overwhelmed. One spectator recalled her tears. "I had the strange sensation that in this gaily dressed little woman before the microphone, I was seeing a living pioneer."[107]

The Shamrock Ball took place for a number of years and featured such Hollywood heavyweights as singer/actress Rhonda Fleming, comedian George Gobel, the Ames Brothers, actress Denise Darcel and singer Eydie Gorme.

With the help of many events such as the ball, the auxiliaries in Houston and Dallas set a goal of raising $600,000 for the endowment fund and met it.

A New Name

The TCHAS board of directors took several important actions at its 1950 annual meeting.

In recognition of her tireless efforts on behalf of the Texas Children's Home and her "babies," the board officially changed the name of the sixty-three-year-old institution to the Edna Gladney Home. More than sixty years later, it still bears her name: the Gladney Center for Adoption. Edna had been the public face of the organization for so many years that few people remembered any other superintendent. She had criss-crossed the country countless times; placed out thousands of infants and children; written untold numbers of letters and notes; raised hundreds of thousands of dollars; comforted an unending parade of young, frightened women; and battled for legislation—she was, in short, already a legend and still had more than a decade of her career left.

Board president A.J. Duncan added his own tribute to the day by giving outright the El Paso Street property and house that he had provided to the Baby Home for more than twenty years. It now owned two of its three locations; a house at 830 Eighth Avenue would soon be purchased for the permanent office.[108] And after the lean war years, the staff had been strengthened, too. Altogether, Edna now oversaw five nurses, four doctors, a hospital manager, a social worker and an application supervisor, plus cooks, laundresses and groundskeepers. In only a few years, she would double the number of nurses, including one African American, and office staff.

In a segregated age, Edna declared, "We only know one race in our work—the human race." Her 1952 Christmas letter listed the ethnic backgrounds of the "many little souls" placed that year: "Jewish, Spanish, Mexican, Italian, Chinese, Negro and European." And though adoptions of older children were becoming increasingly rarer in other facilities, the average age of Edna's placements was eight to ten years old in 1950. Thirty to forty such children arrived every year, brought by parents or relatives who could no longer care for them; they lived in licensed boardinghouses around Fort Worth until placed.

In the mid-1950s, Edna battled once more for new legislation, this time to ensure the same inheritance rights for adoptees as for natural children. That bill passed the Texas legislature in 1957.

Hollywood...Again

The inaugural Shamrock Ball in 1952 was such a success that Dallas parents began thinking how they could honor Edna's years of service. In January 1953, they contacted Greer Garson—now married to Texas oilman Buddy Fogelson—to enlist her help in having Edna appear on the popular television show *This Is Your Life*. The actress was happy to write to host Ralph Edwards and encourage Edna's selection.

Edna was enticed to fly to Los Angeles with TCHAS attorney Sproesser Wynn on the pretense that the trip had to do with publicity for an upcoming *Woman's Home Companion* article on Edna and her work. At the El Capitan Theater on December 16, Edna—under the impression that she was to speak briefly about the Home—was flabbergasted to see Greer Garson in a taped foreword and then to hear Ralph Edwards speak those famous words, "Edna Gladney, this is your life!"

Among the guests were Garland Jones, a suitor of hers from Fort Worth; Reverend Lee Heaton, her minister when Sam died and a longtime friend; a classmate from Milwaukee's Seventh Ward School (whom Edna did not remember at all); one of the first children registered at the Sherman Day Nursery; and a family of now-grown babies she'd placed. Her cousin Mary Owen Routh recalled that Edna felt complimented but did not like surprises and was very uncomfortable. Knowing that she would be, both Mary and Edna's sister, Dorothy Dumas, had declined to appear.

The afterparty was held at the famed Roosevelt Hotel on Hollywood Boulevard. The show and its sponsor, Hazel Bishop cosmetics, presented Edna with a number of gifts: a camera and sound projector, a new Mercury sedan, a music box and a fourteen-carat gold charm bracelet; among the charms were a cradle and a hatbox. (Both the bracelet and the music box are

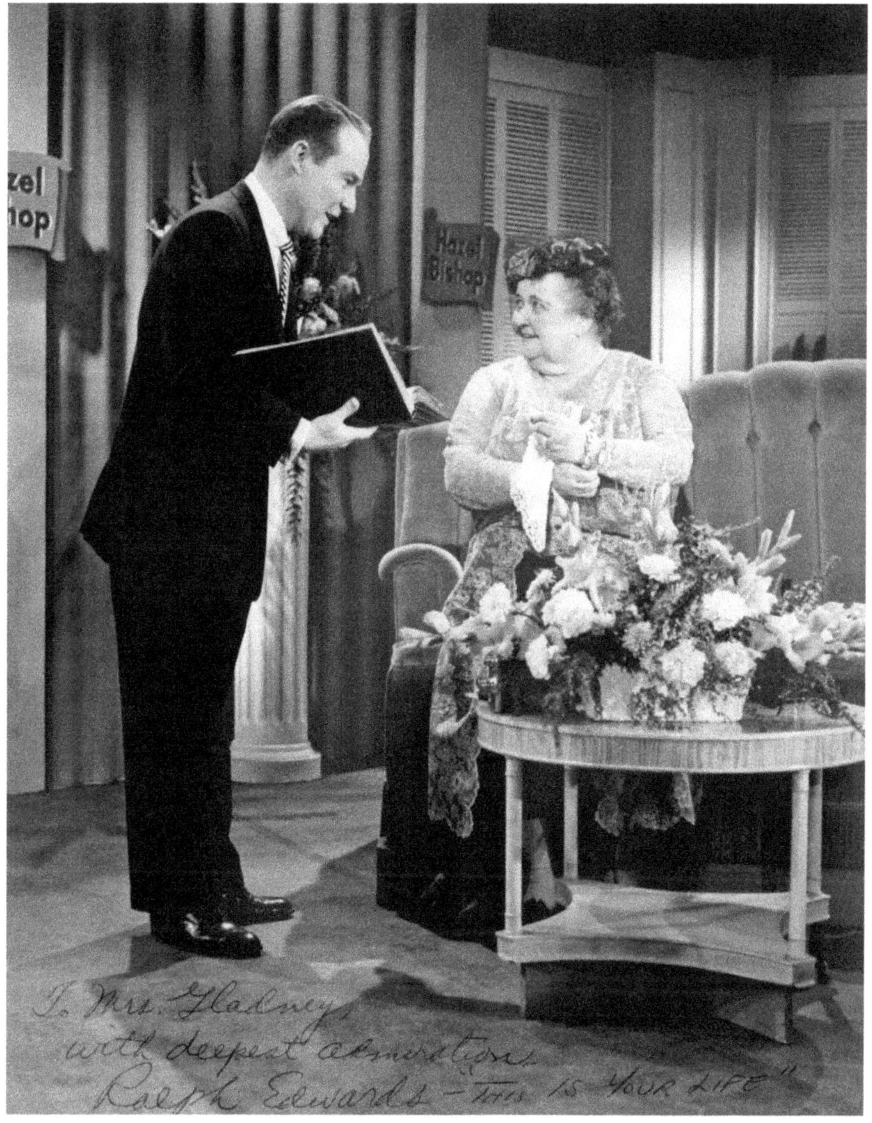

Edna with Ralph Edwards on *This Is Your Life* on December 16, 1953. *Deb Chester Maclin.*

on display in the Gladney Center's exhibit area.) Afterward, Edna was heard to say, "Surprises like this aren't good for an old lady!"

The January 1954 issue of *Woman's Home Companion* on newsstands the following day carried an article by Eleanor Harris titled "I Gave Away 10,000 Babies":

> *Babies without fathers, mothers without husbands—many youngsters hardly out of their teens—these are the people who fill Edna Gladney's world with purpose and love. She gives thousands a better chance in life… She is known as "Aunt Edna" to enough Gladney babies and* [adoptive] *parents to populate a middle-sized American city…At sixty-six years of age she still wears carefully applied eye shadow and mascara day and night; her eyebrows are plucked and penciled. She races through life wearing blue, purple or white dresses under a series of gay little flowered hats and leaving behind her the scent of perfume…Somehow Mrs. Gladney manages to hover like a friendly mother hen over the three units of the Edna Gladney Home and over the lives of everyone involved. She also welcomes a continual flow of "Gladney babies"…who come calling on her.*[109]

The combined effect of the television show and article was the same as with *Blossoms*. Birth mothers came from everywhere in search of Edna Gladney's loving support, so many that she had to add more staff and consider building a new dormitory.

And yet one more movie, also based on a Ralph Wheelwright story, would be made about her and the TCHAS. *All Our Yesterdays* tells the story of a young man who abandons a girl he'd made pregnant and their infant son, only to decide years later, when he'd become a wealthy businessman, to find the boy. He returns to the adoption agency and attempts to get the information he wants, but the administrator refuses to help him, telling him he would be ruining his son's life. He eventually locates the young man but realizes that his son doesn't need him and has a good life with his adoptive family. The story was based on an actual case.

James Cagney played the lead; Helen Hayes was in talks for the administrator's role. Shirley Booth was also considered, but the part eventually went to Barbara Stanwyck. Both she and Cagney were adoptive parents, so they felt strongly about the film and its theme. Walter Pidgeon came "home" again as an attorney. Stage and television actress Betty Lou Keim played a young unwed mother who catches the attention of Cagney's character. And Michael Landon (*Bonanza*) made his film debut in an uncredited part.

Metro-Goldwyn-Mayer was at first disinterested, but Cagney's enthusiasm and personal pitch to executives sold it. Edna's name would be referenced, but otherwise all names and locations were fictitious. Sproesser Wynn expressed concerns that publicity about the Home's unwed mothers often brought protests from adoptive parents, who preferred that the families with whom the children were placed be highlighted.

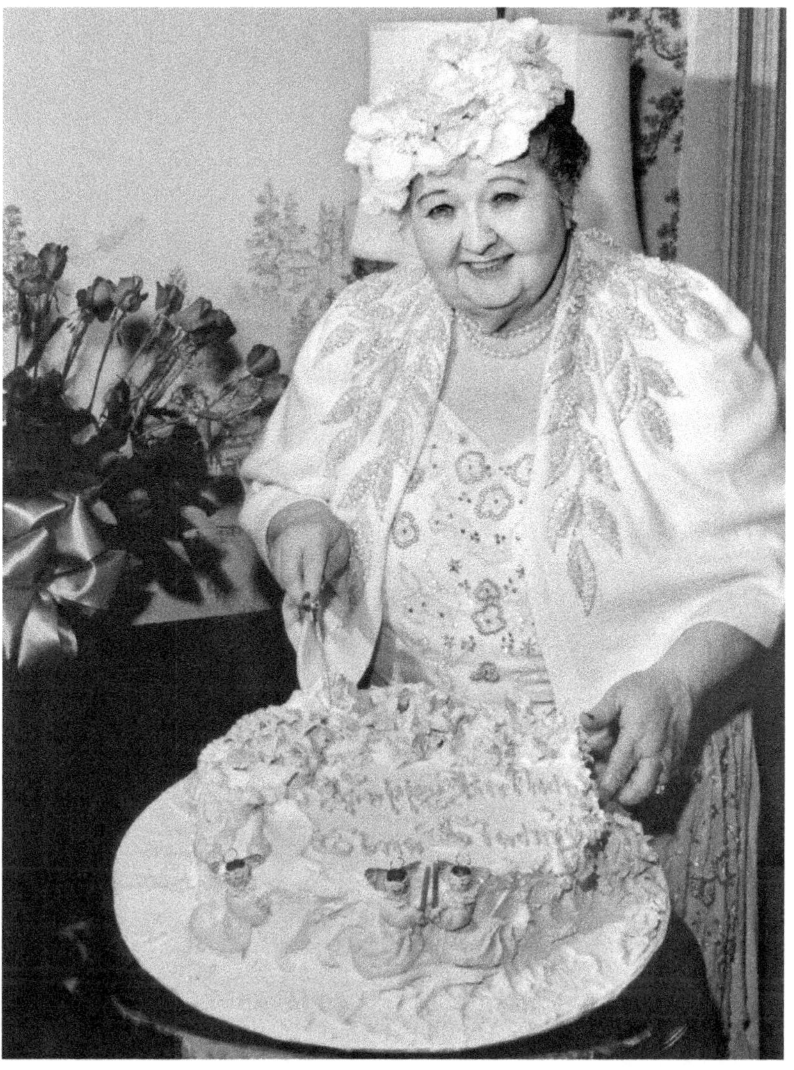

Edna cuts a cake decorated with angels—her signature motif—for her seventieth birthday in 1956. *Deb Chester Maclin.*

Ralph donated $5,000, half his story payment. And Cagney came to Fort Worth in the spring of 1955 to consult with Edna. By the time the film debuted in August 1956, the title had been changed several times, with MGM eventually settling on *These Wilder Years*. Despite a performance by Cagney that many considered among his best, the film fared poorly at the box office and with the critics.

Hometown Honors

Edna enjoyed a singular honor in 1955 when she received two awards from the L.F. Shanblum Lodge of B'nai B'rith for her "benevolence, charity and brotherly love" and also "for outstanding service in community and civic affairs for the general advancement of Americanism and citizenship responsibility."[110] Edna Gladney Home director Marcus Ginsburg presented the awards.

Edna, he said, "is one of those rare people whose very presence radiates confidence, admiration and love...The very nature of her work...dictates that it be done without fanfare and operated almost as secretly as Scotland Yard...Although she would not do so, I personally know that she could name leading bankers, lawyers, doctors, judges, statesmen, financiers, ministers and others who owe their station in life primarily to the home she found for them."[111]

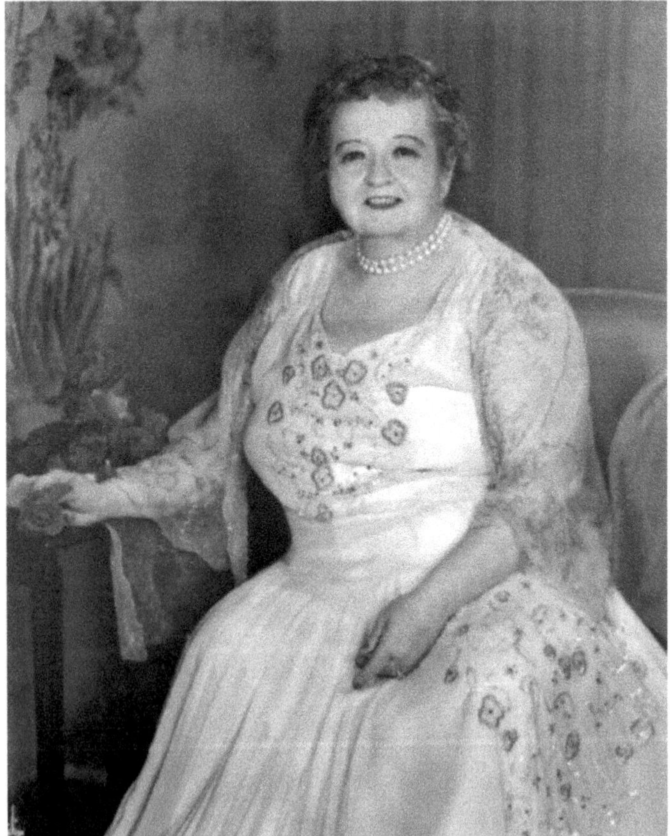

One of the last formal portraits made of Edna, circa 1960. Fort Worth Star-Telegram *Collection, Special Collections, University of Texas–Arlington.*

Among the many telegrams and notes of congratulations she received was one from board member John Steel: "If you keep on, you may be our first woman president."

In 1957, Texas Christian University, where she had studied sociology, also recognized Edna by bestowing on "Fort Worth's angel of mercy" the honorary doctor of laws degree.[112]

"Mrs. Gladney's ministry of mercy," read the citation, "has captured both the imagination and the admiration of the nation…[and is awarded for] for the undying place she has in 10,000 hearts, for the admiration she has earned in millions of lives…for her nurturing of Blossoms in the dust, [and] for her reminder that human life is the supreme of all values."

Edna expressed her gratitude to the trustees. "It will be very difficult for me to accept this honor alone. It has taken everyone from the President of the organization to the gardener, all working together for over sixty years, to make this little sacred organization second to none in the field of child adoption and in mother's care." To friends such as Marcus Ginsburg, she joked, "Had I received an M.D. degree I could have understood it as I have practiced for years without a license." And she wrote to TCU's president, Dr. M.E. Sadler, providing her dress and head size for the robe and mortarboard: "Now dear friend, this is like giving you my last will and testament."

The birth mothers also sent their congratulations. In reply, Edna thanked her "wonderful girls" and wished "for each and every one of you a beautiful and an interesting life and always be interested in someone who needs the load lifted."

Changing Times

As the Edna Gladney Home entered the mid-1950s, it was clear that reorganization within both it and the board of directors was needed to meet new standards for licensing from the State of Texas. A priority was upgrading or rebuilding the aging Baby Home and Hospital; also, the three houses being rented for dorms had been condemned by the fire marshal. Construction and remodeling plans were made, but there were no funds to undertake them; a generous Ford Foundation grant in 1956 enabled hospital construction to begin the following year.[113]

After the death of A.J. Duncan in 1955, Bob Thomas was elected president of the board, which began to rely more on advice provided by the Texas

Department of Public Welfare. To avoid further delays in having department licenses renewed, Edna was forbidden to solicit donations herself but was told to turn over that duty to a financial secretary.

In mid-1956, she was referred to in minutes only as "the Superintendent," not by name, and informed that Public Welfare expected the board and executive committee to operate the Home in strict compliance. Yet the responsibility to see that that happened was placed solely on Edna. Board minutes indicate that she may have been authorizing unbudgeted repairs and capital projects without executive committee approval. But because of Duncan's frequent illnesses and absences before his death, that committee had rarely met.

Perhaps she could see what was coming. In March 1956, Edna drew up several detailed inventories of her personal possessions in all the facilities and her personal library, as well as items that were owned by the "organization." Hundreds of linens and bedding items, furniture, clocks, garden furniture, art works, radios and electric kitchen appliances scattered through the various buildings belonged to her.

The board's new curtness toward Edna came home to roost the winter of 1956–57 when it was publicly rumored that she was very ill—as she indeed was—destitute and unable to pay medical or hospital bills. Edna had worked as superintendent for the first several years with no salary; then she received $150 per month for travel expenses. That eventually became $300 and, in 1953, after more than four decades of volunteer and paid service to the Home, was raised to $500 per month (about $4,380 today). Now, although board officers considered the rumors of destitution to be baseless, they increased her salary to $700 "to put at rest any doubts" and agreed further that, if she ever retired, the board would see that all her reasonable needs were met.

The Child Welfare League (CWL) began a preliminary survey of the facilities and operations as a prelude to a full survey required for membership; the Home had been involved with CWL for decades, and Edna had been a member since 1943. When the final survey was completed in 1959, Edna wept at the findings of outdated facilities and programs spread inefficiently across town. In a later interview, the report's author, Ruby Lee Piester, remembered that at the time, Edna herself was ill, hard of hearing and unable to move around easily. But she admired Edna's "courage and guts" in focusing on the birth mothers, whom society failed to take care of; no one else in the United States was doing similar work.

Those birth mothers knew Edna's good heart. When one requested a wedding ring to wear, Edna put out the call to adoptive parents who were jewelers; they responded immediately. The young woman slipped the ring on and declared she was now married to Aunt Edna. Several birth mothers wrote poems to her.

"To us you are a blessing true / For you have made our gray skies blue." And wrote another, "For you have had the opportunity / Presented to so few. / You have been able to aid many / To rise again after staggering on the road of life."

Even children she'd placed wrote her poetry. "Remember we cried in our early years? / We laid in our cribs, you dried our tears…But now we are older, we won't forget. / The smile on your face. That was it!"

But the times were catching up to Aunt Edna.

Chapter 11

"Our Beloved Leader"

Edna turned seventy-four years old as the new decade of the '60s dawned. Age and ill health were interfering with her executive abilities, but she was so concerned about the new directions being taken by the Edna Gladney Home board that she was reluctant to retire.

"Strenuous Duty"

Matters came to a head in April 1960 when it was announced that she was retiring.[114] Board president Bob Thomas and the executive committee had officially relieved "Mrs. Gladney of the strenuous duty of operating the agency." When her health permitted, Thomas added, she would assist with the campaign to raise money for endowment and a new nursery. The board's decision had been put into action on April 12, the same day that twenty-two employees presented a petition to the board asking that "the management and authority of this organization…be re-directed to Mrs. Gladney." The document cited ten issues, including a decline in income, improper diets given to and improper behavior with birth mothers and termination and threats of termination of longtime employees for no reason.

Thomas had already prepared space for all the babies at the West Texas (now A.J. Duncan) Maternity Hospital and moved them there from El Paso Street by April 15; the old Baby Home would be sold. He had also begun taking over duties as administrator until a new person—"I insist we employ a man for this position."—could be hired. "I know that each of us who love Edna Gladney," he wrote to the executive committee on April 16, "regret that these actions are necessary but in the interest of her health and welfare, we have no alternative…I have been in touch with her every day…She seems to be in accord." In a separate letter to Child Welfare, Thomas reiterated that the board would "choose a competent man with executive experience" to head the seventy-three-year-old organization.

The board hired Walter Delamarter, previously with Texas Baptist social welfare and adoption agencies, to succeed Edna. At first very businesslike with her, he stipulated in his contract that he did not have to call on her for advice, that she had no authority of any kind anymore and that all her official actions had to be approved by him. But he soon succumbed to Edna's charm as so many others had. The Home's Christmas 1960 appeal letter featured a photograph of Edna with the Delamarter family and the assurance that she was "dreaming new dreams and having new visions." In a letter to a friend, she admitted that she'd been a thorn in the side of Bob Thomas.

Edna soon moved from El Paso Street—her residence for more than two decades—to the Chateau de Ville Apartments on Eighth Avenue, near several hospitals. She required nearly round-the-clock care and couldn't travel without a nurse. The Home continued to pay her salary and to help with the cost of care. The board had recently named her president emeritus as an indication of her ongoing status with the institution she'd guided and loved for so long.

"Love Letters to an Angel of Mercy"

In honor of her upcoming seventy-fifth birthday in 1961, the Home collected letters and testimonials from staff, friends and celebrities in a volume entitled "Love Letters to an Angel of Mercy—From a Host of Friends."

One employee recalled how Edna helped the birth mothers: "I've seen you turn their dark yesterdays into bright tomorrows." Another added, "It has been said that no one is indispensable, but in my estimation you are an exception to that rule." Walter Delamarter admitted to feeling "very much like the little boy who struggles along in the snow covered path of his father [trying to walk in his footsteps]…we all know there can never be another Edna Gladney." Even Ralph Edwards (*This Is Your Life*) and

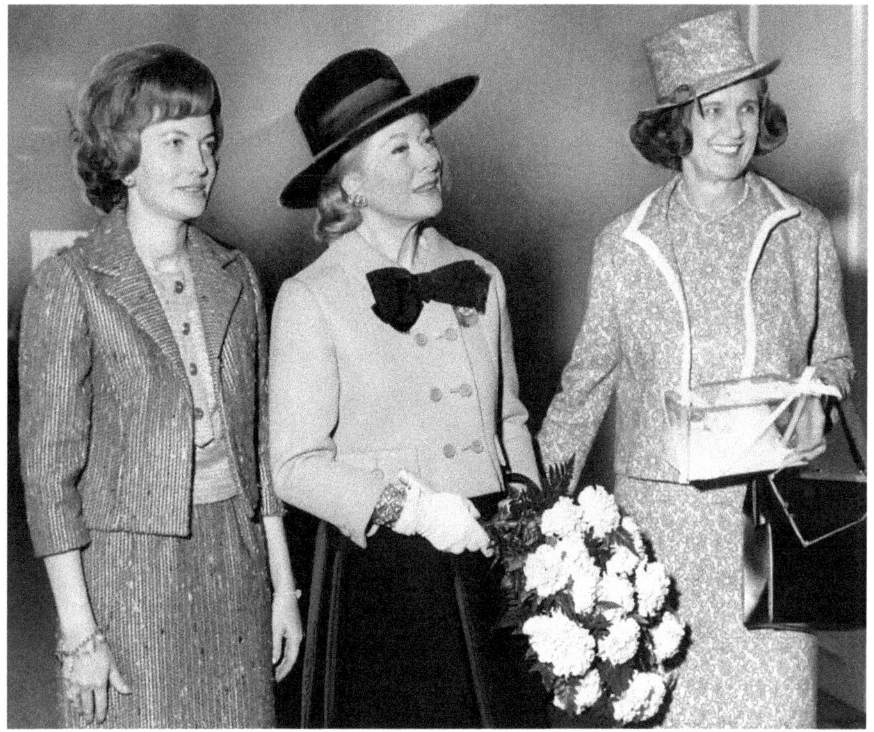

Greer Garson (center) appeared at the Fort Worth Auxiliary's style show and luncheon in 1964. Fort Worth Star-Telegram *Collection, Special Collections, University of Texas–Arlington.*

Greer Garson contributed. Greer also sent a birthday telegram, calling her role as Edna "the most humanly inspiring experience of my whole life, as an actress."

In early February 1961, a testimonial dinner had to be cancelled when Edna went into the hospital with pneumonia. But she rallied as she always had and went back to work, writing letters to help the sick child of an employee, telegraphing good wishes to Jewish adoptive parents on Yom Kippur and checking with another family on the Texas Coast to see if they'd suffered from Hurricane Carla. At the end of September, she was still active, excitedly going over plans for the new nursery with Walter and reminiscing with him about her life. Just a few days later, she lapsed into a coma. True to form, she aroused at least once to tell family and friends, "I'll be all right."

"Our Beloved Leader"

Edna Browning Gladney died just before noon on October 2, 1961, with her sister Dorothy and niece Jane by her side. Walter Delamarter immediately telegraphed board members, telling them, "Our beloved leader and dear friend Aunt Edna passed away" and asking that they serve as honorary pallbearers. "Her final request was that memorial contributions be sent to the Nursery Building Fund instead of flowers." Nevertheless, her funeral book includes eight pages of flowers sent by mourners, including a spray of pink carnations from the birth mothers at the Edna Gladney Home. She was buried next to Sam on October 4 in Rose Hill Cemetery, near Lake Arlington in east Fort Worth.

Newspapers across the country carried news of her passing, including the *Fort Worth Star-Telegram*. "Few deaths, even among the mighty and the prominent in public life, evoke such an outpouring of regret and tribute as has that of Mrs. Edna Gladney…[she] dealt in one of the emotional areas of human relations, and she did so with devotion and compassion."[115] The *Dallas Morning News* reflected, "Human values counted most with Mrs. Gladney and frequently brought clashes with hardpressed agencies to whom welfare work sometimes becomes a numbers game. Mrs. Gladney usually won."[116] And the *Oklahoma City Times* noted that more than one thousand of Edna's "babies" had been placed in that state.

Afterword

The organization's longtime pediatrician, Dr. Edwin G. Schwarz, died in 1962 after a distinguished career. Also that year, the Edna Gladney Home became the first private child welfare agency in Fort Worth to attain membership in the Child Welfare League of America. Ruby Lee Piester became director in 1963 after the departure of Walter Delamarter.

In 1964, the Tarrant County Auxiliary staged its first benefit "Blossoms in the Dust Luncheon and Style Show," which will celebrate fifty years in 2014. Greer Garson came from her Dallas residence to make a surprise appearance; she also visited the busy nursery and exclaimed that she could hear blossoms bawling! She and Edna had remained friends over the years, meeting whenever possible at Neiman-Marcus for lunch. The actress also attended the Edna Gladney Home's centennial in 1987, and after her

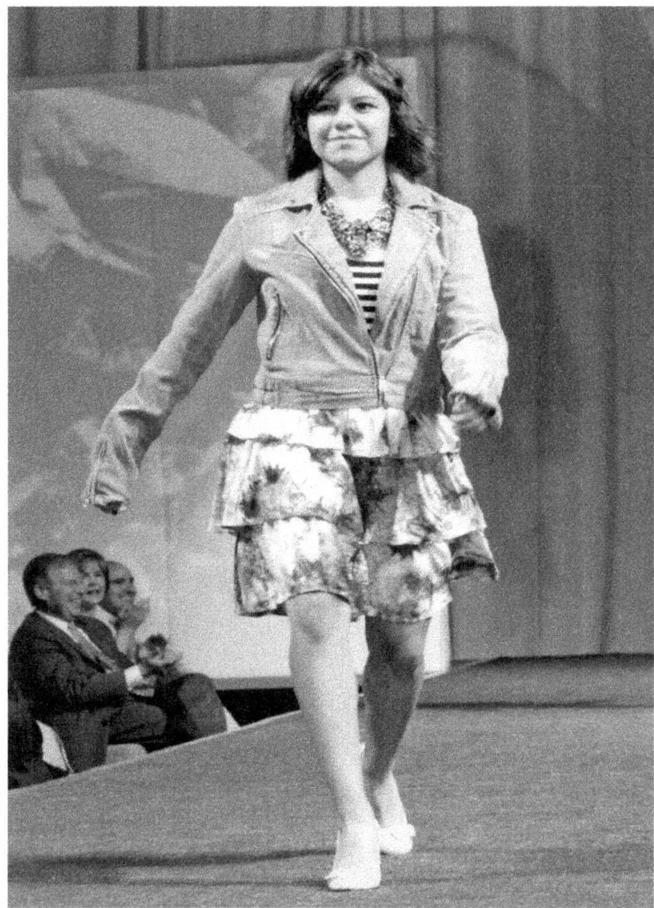

The author's daughter Ann is one of many Gladney "babies" and parents who model in the annual "Blossoms in the Dust Style Show and Luncheon." *Helvey Photography.*

death in 1996, the Greer Garson and Buddy Fogelson Foundation donated $500,000 for birth mothers' educations.

Of the other main *Blossoms in the Dust* constituents, Ralph Wheelwright died in 1971 after writing the Lon Chaney bio film *Man with a Thousand Faces* and doing publicity for *King of Kings*. Walter Pidgeon passed on in 1984 after starring in such classics as *Forbidden Planet*, *Voyage to the Bottom of the Sea* and *Funny Girl*.

Edna's beloved sister Dorothy died in 1981 and her niece Jane in 2006. The author had the great pleasure of knowing Jane Chester and was privileged to be entrusted by her with telling Aunt Edna's story.

The Gladney Center moved from its longtime campus on Hemphill Street in 2002[117] when it broke ground for a new facility in southwest Fort Worth, which features one of the only, if not *the* only, exhibits on adoption history in the country. In 2003, the Hallmark Channel featured the Gladney Center in its series

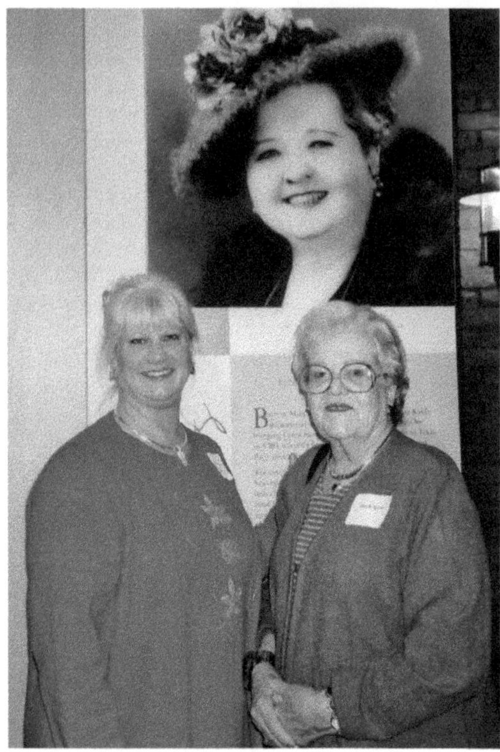

Deb Chester Maclin and her mother, Edna Jane Dumas Chester, at the opening of the Gladney Center's new Visitors Center and historical exhibit in 2002. *Author's collection.*

on adoption; two years later, Edna was honored as a Fort Worth and Texas Legend by Cadillac. Gladney auxiliaries (now Family Associations) and offices span the country and work globally to help orphans. And in 2012, Gladney—the oldest adoption agency in Texas and one of the oldest in the United States—celebrated a milestone that Edna might never have believed would happen: its 30,000th adoption.

As for me, my husband and I enjoy our own beautiful Gladney blossom every day. I often remember a poem that hung in the room near where we met her for the first time. It concluded with these lines: "You were not born under my heart / You were born in it."

She, like so many others, was born in Edna Gladney's heart.

NOTES

CHAPTER 1

1. *Dallas Morning News*, March 30, 1901.
2. *Fort Worth Star-Telegram*, May 5 and 6, 1921.
3. For example, the *Bowie (Texas) Blade* on October 6, 1921.

CHAPTER 2

4. Eleanor Harris, "I Gave Away 10,000 Babies," *Woman's Home Companion*, January 1954, 92.
5. Telephone interview with Mary Owen Routh, April 25, 2010.
6. Letter from Sam to Edna, September 22, 1919.
7. Letter from F.A. Bleger of Lyons, Kansas, to Edna, October 26, 1941. Bleger had worked for Sam at Gladney Milling.
8. Bess Stephenson, "Edna Gladney Is Heroine to Sherman," unknown newspaper, no date.
9. *Sherman Courier*, January 7, 1917, and January 9, 1917; *Sherman Daily Democrat*, January 6, 1917, and January 9, 1917.
10. Stephenson, "Edna Gladney Is Heroine to Sherman."
11. Personal interview with Mary Owen Routh, August 10, 2013.
12. *Sherman Democrat*, May 2, 1921.

CHAPTER 3

13. Piester, *For the Love of a Child*, 12.
14. *Fort Worth Star-Telegram*, November 7, 1920. Edna served as an officer for several terms. Today it is the Women's Service League.
15. Letter from Edna to Louis B. Mayer, January 8, 1942.
16. One of the cowboys in this montage was director Mervyn LeRoy.
17. Dorothy Kahly married Fred Dumas in 1919 in Sherman. Their daughter, Edna Jane, was born there in 1926; the Dumases moved to Fort Worth in 1928.
18. Ralph Wheelwright, "Story Idea for *Blossoms in the Dust*," 9–10.
19. *Dallas Morning News*, September 26, 1955.
20. Pennsylvania Department of Public Health and Charities, *The Degenerate Children of Feeble-Minded Women* (Philadelphia, 1910).
21. By this time, birth certificates were required for military service, passports and some occupations.
22. The phrase has been quoted many times and even turned up in the 2005 book *Dangerous Liaisons: When Cultivated Plants Mate with Their Wild Relatives*.
23. Personal interview with Mary Owen Routh, August 6, 2013.
24. *El Paso Herald*, October 5, 1912.
25. Letter from Edna to Ralph Wheelwright, May 8, 1940. He needed a detailed explanation for script purposes.
26. Addilee Abell Penn (1908–1985) adopted two children with her first husband, George Abell. Her family believes that it was when she saw their birth certificates—stamped illegitimate—that she became involved in changing those documents. She was one of the most important public faces associated with the campaign and later became active with the League of Women Voters, working to tighten the security of Texas voting ballots.
27. Edna's work is recognized on PBS's "Timeline: A History of Adoption in the United States," found on its *American Experience: Daughter from Danang* website.

CHAPTER 4

28. Reverend Lee Heaton was accused of heresy by the Episcopal Church in 1923 after preaching that a belief in the virgin birth as physical fact was not necessary to be a good Christian. The resulting controversy caught him in a fight between fundamentalist and modernist factions;

he was never tried but was publicly rebuked. About 1950, he suffered a heart attack. Edna paid his hospital and medical bills in gratitude for his long friendship.

29. Letter from Edna to Gaylord Stone, March 12, 1936.
30. Letter from Edna to Amon G. Carter, November 25, 1935.
31. *Omaha (NE) World Herald*, December 26, 1936.
32. Texas House Bill 376, Chapter 480, Passed and Effective June 9, 1937.
33. The Home was still accepting older children as late as 1957, long after it had begun to focus on prenatal care of birth mothers.
34. Bureau of Research in the Social Sciences, *Texas' Children: The Report of the Texas Child Welfare Survey* (University of Texas Publication #3837, 1938), 136, 388–92.
35. Edith Alderman Guedry, *Fort Worth Press*, undated column.
36. Edna had wanted to use Schwarz's real name as a tribute to him, but medical ethics prohibited it.
37. At the request of the building's architect and Baby Home board member Wyatt Hedrick, owner Jesse Jones of Houston provided the office rent-free for many years.
38. *Dallas Morning News*, April 21, 1940, and October 2, 1940. While many felt they could become useful Americans as previous European refugees had, there was concern that handicapped, illegitimate or dependent children would become public charges and crowd charitable institutions. In October, the State of Texas allowed refugee children to enter without the bond usually required by public welfare statutes.
39. Wheelwright would also be called on to identify and return to California the body of Carole Lombard, Gable's wife, when she was killed in a 1942 plane crash, returning from a war bond rally tour.
40. Unidentified Fort Worth newspaper, "MGM to Tell Life Story of Fort Worther", April 1940.
41. Letter from Edna to Ralph Wheelwright, June 2, 1940.
42. Wheelwright, "Story Idea," 1.
43. Both Longfellow and Browning have been suggested as sources for the title, but Blind's poem seems to suit best.
44. Wheelwright, "Story Idea," 20.
45. Wheelwright used many ellipses in his text.
46. Wheelwright, "Story Idea," 2.
47. Troyan, *A Rose for Mrs. Miniver*, 112.
48. Edna protested some of the changes: "But it didn't really happen like that!"

49. Letter from Edna to Ralph Wheelwright, June 20, 1940.
50. Letter from Edna to Greer Garson, July 3, 1940.
51. Letter from Greer Garson to Edna, September 25, 1940.
52. Letter from Edna to Ian Hunter, July 3, 1940.

CHAPTER 5

53. Letter from Ralph Wheelwright to Edna, November 7, 1940.
54. Louella Parson column in unidentified newspaper, November 11, 1940.
55. Phone interview with Mary Owen Routh, April 25, 2010.
56. The Ambassador Hotel and most of the Coconut Grove were demolished about 2005.
57. *Fort Worth Star-Telegram*, November 15, 1987.
58. Letter from Anita Loos to Edna, December 5, 1940.
59. Letter from Mervyn LeRoy to Edna, December 13, 1940.
60. *Oakland Tribune*, April 20, 1941.
61. *Danville (VA) Bee*, February 3, 1941.
62. *Shamokin (PA) News-Dispatch*, August 13, 1941.
63. Some of these photographs survive in Special Collections at UCLA's Young Research Library.
64. Harris, "I Gave Away 10,000 Babies," 94.
65. Letter from Dr. Grace Humphrey Hood to Louis B. Mayer, July 5, 1941
66. Letter from Edna to Guy Yowell of the *Sherman Democrat*, April 15, 1941.
67. Letter from Clarissa Lehman to Irving Asher, February 10, 1941.
68. *Fort Worth Star-Telegram*, June 22, 1941.

CHAPTER 6

69. Dennis R. Smith, "Babies a Major Film Problem," *Canton (OH) Repository*, March 30, 1941. Babies 30 to 89 days old made fifty dollars, and those 91 to 180 days made twenty-five dollars.
70. Ibid.
71. Wheelwright, "Story Idea," 20–23.
72. Loos, *Kiss Hollywood Good-bye*, 172–73.
73. Patricia worked in several more movies, including *Presenting Lily Mars* with Judy Garland and *Frenchman's Creek*.
74. "Press Book," courtesy of University of Southern California Cinematic Arts Library.

75. The three presidents and Lloyd George were "half-orphans," with one parent dead. Sunday's father died, and his mother was so poor that she sent her youngest to an orphanage. Washington's white father is unknown, and his mother died when he was small. Audubon was illegitimate; his mother died after he was born, and he was later formally adopted by his birth father and his wife. Carver was also born a slave, his father unknown; he and his mother were kidnapped when he was young. Only he was recovered. Both of Poe's parents died when he was young, and he was taken in and raised by the Allans. Roosevelt was orphaned by the time she was ten.
76. Letter from Charles Kassel to Louis B. Mayer, June 28, 1941.

Chapter 7

77. "Hedda Hopper's Hollywood," unidentified and undated newspaper clipping.
78. Carey, *All the Stars in Heaven*, 254.
79. Accounting for inflation, $21 then is approximately $350 today.
80. *San Antonio Light*, February 16, 1942.
81. Letter from Ralph Wheelwright to Edna, June 1941.
82. Letter from Louis B. Mayer to Edna, June 18, 1941.
83. *Dallas Morning News*, "Woman's World," September 4, 1941.
84. Letter from Ralph Wheelwright to Edna, July 10, 1941.
85. *Lancaster (WI) Independent*, July 17, 1941, and letter from Greer Garson to Edna, December 15, 1941.
86. Neither woman had children.

Chapter 8

87. Letter from Ralph Wheelright to Edna, January 1942.
88. *Fort Worth Star-Telegram*, December 29, 1941.
89. Undated, unidentified newspaper, probably from Baltimore.
90. *Dallas Morning News*, September 4, 1941.
91. Letter from Edna to Louis B. Mayer, January 8, 1942.
92. Letter from Louis B. Mayer to Edna, January 29, 1942.
93. Louella Parsons column, *Greensboro (NC) Daily News*, November 15, 1942.

94. Letter from Ralph Wheelwright to Edna, July 6, 1942.
95. Letter from Ralph Wheelwright to Edna, November 4, 1942.
96. *Dallas Morning News*, August 23, 1942.
97. Undated letter from Dr. Jack W. Amesse to Edna, probably 1943.
98. Letter from Ralph Wheelwright to Edna, August 19, 1943. Ralphie died of leukemia in 1952, and in his memory, Ralph became involved with a Boston research center. The Wheelwrights also adopted a son, John.
99. Other members of the troupe included Judy Garland, Kathryn Grayson, Harpo Marx and Dick Powell.

CHAPTER 9

100. Christmas card from Edna to Mr. and Mrs Larry Oles, December 21, 1944.
101. *Dallas Morning News*, January 7, 1945.
102. Ibid., October 12, 1947.

CHAPTER 10

103. The name was changed in 1955 to A.J. Duncan Memorial Hospital to honor his memory.
104. "*Blossoms in the Dust* Heroine Visits Home of Adopted Tots." An unidentified Los Angeles newspaper, circa 1950, called this an "experiment," indicating few other organizations were doing a program like it.
105. Katherine Ferber, "With Love from Aunt Edna," *Viewpoint* (Junior League of Oakland-East Bay, 1981).
106. Forty-three brick masons donated a day each to lay brick on the recreation building; plumbers, electricians and others donated time, too. The structure opened in the spring of 1954.
107. Eleanor Harris, "I Gave Away 10,000 Babies," 94.
108. Edna and the Home's board wanted to consolidate all divisions into one campus, but the cost was too high.
109. Eleanor Harris, "I Gave Away 10,000 Babies," 34, 92. This article was reprinted in *Reader's Digest* in February 1954.
110. *Fort Worth Star-Telegram*, November 15, 1955.
111. Typescript of his remarks found in Edna's papers.

112. President Dwight D. Eisenhower was to have delivered the commencement address and received an honorary degree that day, too, but an emergency kept him in Washington.
113. Famed Texas architect and board member Wyatt Hedrick donated much time on construction plans.

Chapter 11

114. In letters to several friends, she wrote, "I have *been* retired (author's italics)."
115. *Fort Worth Star-Telegram,* October 2, 1961.
116. *Dallas Morning News,* October 4, 1961.
117. After Edna's death, the Home was consolidated on Hemphill Street around the maternity hospital.

Bibliography

Archives and Manuscripts

Fort Worth Public Library: Genealogy and Local History: newspaper microfilm, city directory, vertical files.

Gladney Center for Adoption archives: records, photographs, scrapbooks.

Gladney, Edna. Personal and professional papers, photographs, newspaper clippings, publications, movie scripts, books and related documents. Private collection.

Houston Metropolitan Research Center: Elizabeth Robertson: "Edna Gladney: Texas' Greatest Humanitarian." 1958. Typescript.

Sherman (Texas) Public Library: genealogy records, newspapers, city directory.

Tarrant County Archives (Fort Worth): Mary Daggett Lake Collection, court records.

Tarrant County: district court records.

University of California–Los Angeles: MGM Research Department Files: Blossoms in the Dust Production Book: Boxes 8, 46 and 47.

University of Houston: (1) Planned Parenthood of Houston and Southeast Texas, Series 1. (2) Minnie Fisher Cunningham Papers, Subseries 2, Texas Equal Suffrage Association (Reports and Correspondence).

University of Southern California: Cinematic Arts Library: MGM Press Book for *Blossoms in the Dust*, 1950 re-issue.

University of Texas at Arlington: Special Collections: photographs, vertical files.

Books

Bureau of Research in the Social Sciences. *Texas' Children: The Report of the Texas Child Welfare Survey*. Austin: University of Texas Publication #3837, 1938.

Carey, Gary. *All the Stars in Heaven: Louis B. Mayer's MGM*. New York: Dutton, 1981.

Fessler, Ann. *The Girls Who Went Away: The Hidden History of Women Who Surrendered Children for Adoption in the Decades Before* Roe v. Wade. New York: Penguin Press, 2006.

Green, Nathan C., ed. *Story of the 1900 Galveston Hurricane*. Baltimore, MD: R.H. Woodward Co., 1900. Re-issued by Pelican, 2000.

Hart, Hastings H., ed. *Preventive Treatment of Neglected Children*. Vol. 4. New York: Russell Sage Foundation, 1910. (Google Books)

Loos, Anita. *Kiss Hollywood Good-bye*. London: W.H. Allen, 1974.

Newspaper Artists' Association. *Makers of Fort Worth*. Fort Worth, TX: Newspaper Artists' Association, 1914.

Pennsylvania Department of Public Health and Charities. *The Degenerate Children of Feeble-Minded Women*. Philadelphia, 1910. (Google Books).

Piester, Ruby Lee. *For the Love of a Child: The Gladney Story: 100 Years of Adoption in America.* Austin, TX: Eakin Press, 1987.

State Department of Public Welfare. *Laws Relating to Adoptions in Texas*. Austin, TX, 1967.

Troyan, Michael. *A Rose for Mrs. Miniver*. Lexington: University Press of Kentucky, 2005.

Articles

de Grandchamp, Aline. "Girls Get New Start in Home." *Christian Science Monitor*, September 30, 1957.

Guthrie, Chris, and Joanna L. Grossman. "Adoption in the Progressive Era: Preserving, Creating, and Re-Creating Families." *American Journal of Legal History* 43, no. 3 (July 1999).

Harris, Eleanor. "I Gave Away 10,000 Babies." *Woman's Home Companion,* January 1954.

"Welfare Worker." *The Texas Digest* 17, no. 19 (May 10, 1941).

Bibliography

Government Publications

United States Census: Wisconsin and Texas, 1840–1940.

Electronic Databases

GenealogyBank.com
Handbook of Texas Online: tshaonline.org
Legislative Reference Library of Texas: lrl.state.tx.us
Portal to Texas History: texashistory.unt.edu

INDEX

E

F

G

H

T

U

W

About the Author

Sherrie S. McLeRoy received a bachelor of arts degree in history/anthropology with high honors in anthropology from Sweet Briar College and is a 1976 graduate of the Williamsburg Seminar for Historical Administrators. Her first career, from 1974 to 1988, was as a museum administrator/curator in Virginia and Texas. Since then, she has been a writer, speaker and independent historical scholar. She has written or contributed to more than twenty books on the histories of Texas and her native Virginia. From 2000 to 2002, she was a consultant/researcher/writer on an exhibit about the history of the Gladney Center for Adoption.

www.ingramcontent.com/pod-product-compliance
Lightning Source LLC
LaVergne TN
LVHW021155160826
845679LV00024B/2124